TOGETHER

THOUGHTS AND STORIES
ABOUT LIVING IN COMMUNITY

JEFF HAMPTON

© 2021

Published in the United States by Nurturing Faith, Macon, GA.

Nurturing Faith is a book imprint of Good Faith Media (goodfaithmedia.org).

Library of Congress Cataloging-in-Publication Data is available.

ISBN: 978-1-63528-132-3

All Scripture citations are from the New Revised Standard Version (NRSV)
unless otherwise indicated.

CONTENTS

Church and the Kingdom: 85
Kindred Spirits

PREFACE

I never intended to write a book about "community"—what that word means and what living in community means and looks like. With the advent of social media, I was invited by the associate pastor at my church to be one of several bloggers to offer weekly thoughts that would be posted on the church's Facebook page. I jumped on the opportunity and seized it as a challenge to have a submission every week.

At the risk of sounding boastful, while other bloggers have come and gone or have been more sporadic, I have submitted something every week. The only deviation from that has been when the associate pastor has placed us on hiatus to provide other offerings during Advent and Lent. Even then, I've continued to post thoughts on my own website. I've now been doing this consistently for almost ten years.

For me it has been a writing challenge, probably coming out of my training and early work as a newspaper reporter where, if I wasn't assigned something every day, I was challenged and encouraged to find good stories to tell. More important, it's been a spiritual stretching of sorts. Some readers have called it a ministry. That may be true; that's for them and now you to decide. But for me, the act of working out my thoughts at a keyboard has forced me to explore what I believe and whether or not I practice what I preach.

In the midst of this, we've made an interesting discovery. I say "we," because my wife LeAnn suggested that I gather some of these writings in a book. She went back and began rereading them all, noting what she thought were the strongest and categorizing them by general topic. And that's when we discovered that an overwhelming and recurring theme in these writings—week after week, year after year—has been community. Not "community" as defined by the census bureau and the chamber of commerce, but rather all the different types of community we live in. That includes family, friends, neighbors, churches, workplaces, towns, states, countries, races, and humankind. At different times we all live and interact in these communities—usually in several simultaneously.

The question then—and what these writings seem to ask—is how do we live in these communities? Are we contributors or detractors? Do we bring good or harm? Are we active or do we watch from the sidelines? What is our role for better or for worse?

The writings that follow pose these questions. Sometimes I suggest answers, sometimes I only hint at answers, and quite often I simply stir the conversation. I do this with personal stories and observations; sometimes the point is obvious, and sometimes it is resting between the lines. My hope in your reading is that you will join the conversation in whatever way you wish. I'm not asking you to go out and join a community. You don't need to because you're already a member—of several, in fact. Instead, consider your place in your communities, your roles, what that means to them, and what that means to you.

—Jeff Hampton

ACKNOWLEDGMENTS

To LeAnn Kite Hampton, my wife and best friend, who was the first person to suggest that I actually publish something, and who was the true impetus behind this project.

To Mark Wingfield, my associate pastor and friend who graciously provided the weekly forum in which these writings first appeared and who let me say whatever I wanted to say.

To Alison Wingfield, my go-to editor and proofreader for this book and others who, with Mark, has been an encourager and promoter.

To the community of Wilshire Baptist Church and the many readers beyond who have been my steady online audience and who have encouraged my thoughts with their words and emojis.

FAMILY AND FRIENDS: FLESH AND BLOOD

When I first opened my eyes on the morning I was born, my family was there. I didn't choose them, and for a long time I was compelled by nature and nurture and even the law to live with them, but at some point I made the conscious decision to stick with them. They were mine, and I was theirs. Over the years, I've gathered a few close friends and lovers who have become my family too.

The first community we know is the family we are born into. That can be a source of great joy or deep sorrow because this is the community that most forms us for better or for worse. We don't get to choose this community, but we can choose how we will interact and live in it. And we can invite new members into the fold.

Family Ties

It was a day I'll never forget: the day we said goodbye to Kenneth Wallace, age ninety-four. He was my great uncle on the family tree, but he was my *great* uncle because of who he was.

My parents were both only children, so we didn't have any regular aunts and uncles, but my grandparents had lots of siblings and Kenny was the youngest. And because he and my great aunt Lucy had no children, they doted on their nephews and nieces and great nephews and nieces. Lucy was the life of the party and made us giggle and laugh till we were sick, while Kenny had a quiet, gentle strength and an ever-present smile that was equally magnetic. Steady, calm, and consistent—he may be the most "together" person I've ever known.

As I grew up and began to experience life's twists and turns, Kenny became a role model in two unexpected ways. With no children of my own, I found myself wanting to emulate Kenny and at least be a good uncle. I doubt that I've measured up, but it's a role I've always tried to take seriously. And then when Kenny lost his dear Lucy after more than fifty years together, I saw him hold his head high, lean on his faith and family, and keep getting up every day and getting the most out of whatever life had to offer. It wasn't long before God blessed him with a wonderful new love and companion. When life took me down that same path, it was Kenny I wanted to emulate again.

When Kenny died, I drove with my brother and his son—my nephew—the 230 miles to East Texas for his funeral. It was a good trip with lots of good conversation, some of it serious and some of it just silly. And while we were deep in the Piney Woods where cell signals are weak, my nephew got an unexpected call from his brother—my oldest nephew—a Marine in Afghanistan. I was pleased when he asked to speak to me, and I was handed the phone.

I didn't say much, just a simple "How ya doin'?" and "I'm thinkin' 'boutcha." That's what Uncle Kenny would have said.

Every Moment

As I was writing one day, a friend was spending perhaps his last day with his mother. It was a heartbreaking time, but also an important time—a holy time.

I'm at an age when many people I know are going through this with parents, spouses, brothers, and sisters. Having been through the death of a spouse, I know these are sad days, but they also are rich days. They are days of humble privilege and responsibility as you help your loved one move on.

Therefore, I have some advice: Be there for every moment that you can. Work and other activities will wait for you; this time is too important to miss. Stay close, stay up all night if you must. Lean on family and friends for strength when the days get long and the emotional weight gets heavy. Most importantly, trust your loved one to God's timing and mercy. And trust, too, that God will help you sort through the memories, softening the difficult ones and brightening the sweet ones.

Almost Left Behind

"We forgot the refrigerator!" We realized that hours after we'd moved out of the house and moved everything to an apartment and storage. We went back for it the next day. Our realtor laughed and said it's not unusual for people who are moving to leave things behind, such as dishwashers full of dishes. The mover who came back to put the fridge into storage said he'd seen people leave attics full of boxes of belongings.

Life is full of comings and goings, gatherings and leavings. Sometimes we gather things out of need, but sometimes it's just plain greed. Sometimes we leave things out of hasty forgetfulness, but sometimes it's out of willful separation. We do it with possessions, and we do it with people.

And then there comes a day for each of us when we leave everything behind. Recently I attended two funerals—one for a forty-six-year-old who left us far too soon, and the other for an eighty-five-year-old who lived a long fulfilling life. Both left behind possessions, but both also left us with memories to cherish.

I like what musician Don McLean said about it: "The book of life is brief, / And once the page is read, / All but love is dead, / That is my belief."[1]

Years ago, when we cleaned out my grandparents' house, we were getting ready to drive away when we realized the brass door knocker engraved with my grandfather's name was still on the front door. We grabbed a screwdriver, loosened it, and took it with us. It would mean nothing to the next occupants, but to us it represented a wonderful life and all the relationships that were entwined with it.

Love and relationships are for keeps.

In Praise of Fathers (in-Law)

I don't care much for those Father's Day cards that stipulate "Dear Father-in-Law . . ." because it sounds so legalistic. It's true that the role of father-in-law is created by the legal marriage contract between two people, but I prefer to buy cards that just say "Father" or "Dad." That's because I was blessed to have two wonderful fathers (in-law).

Popular culture paints the father-in-law as a strict, overbearing man who puts the son-in-law on notice that he will never be good enough for his daughter. Perhaps no one portrayed that better than Robert DeNiro in the *Meet the Parents* film and its sequel. Those movies were comedies, but I know real men who have lived under that kind of pressure from their wives' fathers. Not me.

First came Dick Wearden, who accepted my Baptist ways in his devout Catholic family and always focused on our common faith rather than our different practices. For twenty-five years he gave me the love and respect of a favored son. When Debra, his daughter, became ill, he helped me stand strong. And later, when I married LeAnn, Dick was sitting near the front of the church to bless my new beginning. That's the father he was.

And then there was Perry Kite, who greeted me with a hearty handshake and a friendly chuckle the first time we met. He provided constant support and encouragement during the years as I grew to know and love his daughter. He was our biggest cheerleader as we took on some ambitious projects such as building a house—as newlyweds. That's the father he was.

As for my own father, one of the greatest gifts he has given me has been to be a loving father (in-law) to both Debra and LeAnn. What's more, he accepted Dick and Perry as brothers in the mission of seeing that we're safe, happy, and loved. When Dick passed, Dad didn't hesitate to make the three-hundred-mile trip to pay his respects. That's the father he is.

Next time Father's Day comes around, don't forget to show some appreciation for your father (in-law) if you have one. And if you are a father (in-law), know that the role you play is much more important than just that legalistic "in-law" thing.

Lessons from Mothers

Mother's Day always causes me to reflect on the many gifts and lessons I have received from my mothers over the years. Following are three collected on one particular day.

Watch out for those earthly treasures.

I'll start at the end, on a Sunday evening during a Mother's Day cookout at our house, when my mother called her two sons out into the yard for a lawn-chair summit. For a few fleeting seconds I was concerned about what the topic might be. And then she said, "It's time . . . to quit paying rent on the storage unit."

Whew! Nothing so dire after all. Still, a daunting task: to sort through furniture and odds and ends saved from generations of Hamptons and McKenzies and decide what should be kept for future generations, what should be donated or sold, and what should just be discarded.

Mom has always treasured relationships more than possessions—she wanted family time more than gifts each year—so the cleanout went pretty smoothly. It wasn't as immediate as it might have been, but we made some new memories as we made decisions on "trash vs. treasure," divided out what needed to stay in the family, donated to worthy causes, and ultimately closed out the storage unit.

Live every day to the fullest.

Earlier in the day I had an unusual conversation with my mother-in-law. The subject was two-cycle engines—the type that are on lawn trimmers and require a mix of gasoline and oil. It's a conversation that men might have, but Thelma is a take-charge, hands-on woman, and when she had a question about the oil, I was glad I could provide an answer.

More than that, I was glad to be reminded how important it is to be engaged every day. At ninety-seven, Thelma is a living reminder that life is what you make of it, and the more you do, the more you live. She teaches Mother's Day Out at her church, pokes around in the yard, teaches Sunday school, and speaks her mind fearlessly. There's no "stop" in her, and I love being around her.

Faith is the tie that binds.

On the Saturday before Mother's Day, I had a nice phone call from my other mother-in-law. Terri called to thank me for the card and letter I sent, and then just to talk because, as she said, "We'll always be family." In our Bible study class, we'd been studying the Old Testament book of Ruth, where Naomi and her daughter-in-law have both lost spouses but are bound together by faith. My relationship with Terri has that "Ruth and Naomi" quality to it because our shared faith is the real family tie that binds.

Empty Nests

LeAnn and I have no children, but we have known the empty nest in a way. For three weeks one spring we watched in wonder as a pair of doves took over one of our hanging ferns on the front porch to lay eggs, sat on them until they hatched, and nurtured two baby doves until they were ready to fly.

We watched as the adults took turns sitting on the eggs, then shielding the hatchlings from weather and predators, and feeding them from beak to beak. We watched the little ones grow—from naked, skeletal caricatures with closed eyes and oversized beaks, to down-covered bodies with spiked head feathers, to sleek young doves preening and preparing their wings for flight. So fascinated were we that we set up a "dove cam" just inside the window so we could capture images of their rapidly changing development.

We didn't see the youngsters take their first leaps from the nest, but we watched as they stretched and fluttered their wings for the first time and briefly lifted a few centimeters above the nest. Later, we saw them walking in the flower bed and then leap up to the porch railing where they struggled to keep their balance like children learning to ride a bike for the first time. When we went out to look at them more closely, the mother darted across the yard and into the street where she skittered along the ground to mimic a wounded bird, as if to say, "Come after me, but leave my children alone."

And then one afternoon they were all gone. We watched for them but didn't recognize them among the dozens of doves that live in the trees around us. We missed them, but we had plenty of photos and memories.

We've witnessed the cycle several times since then with doves and even finches. We're always captivated, but we know our empty nests are trivial compared to what friends have experienced. There's Julie, who said goodbye to her son who was born with a rare genetic birth defect but who soared like an eagle every day that he had because his mother nurtured, encouraged, and empowered him to be all that God intended him to be. Then there are friends who have watched as their daughters and sons left their nests to fly away with their life companions. Their weddings overflowed with love and joy because the new couples had been nourished and raised on the fruits of the Holy Spirit and taught by their parents to fly with God as their guide.

In Matthew 6:26, we read the familiar words of Jesus: "Look at the birds of the air; they do not sow or reap or store away in barns, and yet your heavenly Father feeds them. Are you not much more valuable than they?"

We all occupy nests of sorts, and at different times those we love must leave for whatever reason, and we do the same. But no matter where we are, no matter where we fly, God is watching over us. If mother doves watch over their hatchlings, and human parents do the same for their children, then how much more does our God and creator love and care for us?

Taking a break from thinking about this, I went out on the back porch for a little while and noticed that the sounds of birds flying around the birdfeeder were accompanied by the laughter of children at the church playground nearby. Our nest on the front porch may be empty, but there still are birds everywhere.

Families and Saints

Sitting at a holiday bazaar selling books, one thing was evident as we watched masses of people walk by: There's no denying the power of DNA and genetics. All day we saw groups of people who looked so much alike it was almost scary. This was most noticeable among women, with mothers and daughters and sisters ranging in ages from teens to octogenarians revealing amazing family resemblances.

Each of us carries the genetic material of those who created us. On the outside those genes determine the shape of our nose, the set and color of our eyes, the tint and texture of our hair. Our bloodlines dictate our hairlines and waistlines, our freckles and moles. I have my mother's blue eyes and fair skin and my father's stature and build, along with his full head of hair that began turning gray in our thirties.

The story is the same on the inside. Anyone who has started with a new doctor has answered all the questions about family medical history. Blood pressure, cholesterol levels, tendencies for certain cancers and serious diseases—they all have a starting point in those who came before us. There's not much we can do but be grateful for the good stuff and vigilant about the bad.

When it comes to personality and character traits, there's much debate about the impact of nature versus nurture on how we behave, who we befriend, what we believe. As with the shape of my ears and the length of my toes, I have my parents and their parents to thank for the best parts of my personality.

And the worst parts? I once thought I had my mother's handwriting, but the one time I tried to use it to cut a corner in school I got busted. We laugh at the infraction now because it was so outside the character that was modeled for me from day one: My parents aren't cheaters, and it turns out neither am I.

All Saints Day always makes me mindful of the saints who have shaped me—physically, socially, spiritually—and those who have been patient with me and continue to be so. I'm not perfect, yet, and I know I never will be. But I'm not done yet either, and none of us ever are.

Our challenge, then, is to help bring out the best in each other and help each other overcome the worst—whether we are families in the flesh or siblings in the spirit.

Father and Son

"How's your dad?"

"He has Parkinson's, and it's not any fun."

That was the give-and-take between me and my friend Ken for several years when I would ask about his father, Bob. The answer was honest and brief, and it was given by a son who loved his father so much and knew his father so well. You see, Bob was an electrical engineer, and I've known enough engineers to know that he would have appreciated Ken's precision and brevity.

I don't know exactly what Bob did during his career; I know he worked with some of the earliest computers, and I recall a Saturday when he took Ken and me to his office and let us type commands into a computer. It was nothing compared to what computers can do today, but in that day a machine talking back to us with words on a screen was fantastic.

I know more about what Bob did at home and in the community. He turned spare parts and household items into TV antennas and satellite dishes. He drove a VW Beetle with the enthusiasm of a man who loved its simple mechanical design. He was a behind-the-scenes, go-to guy at his church, especially for audio-visual and electronic matters.

A few times when our home TV went dark, Bob would come with his gear and test the vacuum tubes one by one until he found the culprit that had gone bad. In the decades following his diagnosis, I never heard Bob talk about his disease, but I'm guessing he approached it the same way he handled everything else: quietly, methodically, honestly.

Ken's description of his father's struggle, likewise, was honest because as a psychologist he knows how these relationships should work. When I was going through my own trials, he advised that the person with the illness gets to set the tone for how it will be addressed. If they want to talk about it openly, then that's the way it should be. If they want to be silent, that's fine. If they want to punctuate their struggle with humor, that's okay.

In his final years, Bob was known to smile and whisper "mission accomplished" when completing what was once a simple task, and that was part of his personality too. He was a master of the one-liner and the groaner pun. He often would comment or answer with a line from an old song or a movie. He could express pleasure with nothing more than a smile and could discipline his children—and me by association—with a few softly spoken words.

Following Ken's counsel, I believe we best love the ones we love when we let them continue to be themselves even as they are losing themselves and we are grieving. It's tempting to try to make it better or more comfortable and manageable for ourselves, but it's an act of tender mercy and love to let them leave the way they lived.

Bob left this life just two days after his eighty-fourth birthday. He was a man of strong but quiet faith, and we have faith that his spirit is no longer trapped inside his failing body. I think Ken might say it this way:

"How's your dad?"

"He's free."

Sacred Ground

"You're living on sacred ground." That's what I told our friend who had learned her husband would not survive cancer. "It doesn't feel like it," she cried, and LeAnn and I cried with her. "But that's what it is," I said.

The sacred ground of living with someone who is dying is an idea first planted in my head by the hospice chaplain assigned to us when my first wife, Debra, was dying with cancer. He said, "Whenever we enter a home where a family is walking with a loved one to the next stage of their journey, we are entering sacred ground."

I had never thought of it in that way, but it felt like it to me because it was a place where heaven and earth meet. We watch as the person who is leaving begins to think and live more spiritually than physically. We help as much as we can, in whatever way they request, but the transformation is not happening to us and so there is only so much we can do. We stand on the earthly edge of what we know and try to hold on while at the same time trusting and letting go.

Not long after Debra left, I was reflecting with her father on what we had been through and I told him, "This is the most important thing I have ever done . . . and may ever do." I was talking about standing on that sacred ground with his daughter. It might have been hyperbole, but that's what it felt like at the time.

After visiting with our friend and watching her drive away, LeAnn and I turned to go back up the sidewalk flanked by a beautiful blanket of snapdragons and tulips. I realized then that I am still living on sacred ground, and unexpectedly so.

You see, anytime we tie our lives to another and vow to share our joys and sorrows and everything else that life brings, we're living on sacred ground. How we treat that other person, whether in the worst of times or the best of times, is a direct reflection of how we believe God loves us—or doesn't. And so, while I stood on sacred ground with Debra through twenty-five years and those difficult last months, my relationship with God didn't end on the morning she left. He let me go to my knees for a while and in fact knelt there with me, but then He stood me up again, dusted me off, and pointed me in a new direction and toward a new piece of sacred ground.

It's a quarter-acre lot in downtown Garland with LeAnn, but more than that it is the minutes and days and years we may have together. And we know that we are not the ones who make this ground sacred. That is the work of God.

Love on a Stick

"Who wants a Fudgsicle?" That's what Dad asked enthusiastically from the kitchen on a visit with my parents. It was a familiar question, and I readily responded as I always have: "I do."

When I was a kid it wasn't unusual for Dad to stop at the neighborhood 7-Eleven to cash a check and pick up whatever else was needed. And more often than not, especially on Sunday nights after church, he'd come out of the store with all of that and a handful of Fudgsicles. In case you aren't familiar, Fudgsicles are chocolate ice cream bars on a stick and once were sold individually in big floor freezers at convenience stores. Maybe they still are.

When we got home, we'd sit around the kitchen table and Dad would hand out the Fudgsicles, which we'd unwrap and eat. It became one of those unremarkable family traditions that you don't really notice until you've not done it for years and your father suddenly invites you to indulge again. But back then it was such a regular thing that on one occasion after my sister died, we gasped a little when, as Dad passed out the ice cream bars, he realized he had bought five when only four were needed.

That was on my mind one recent night as I ate the Fudgsicle in the same way I did as a kid. I nibbled down one side and then down the other until I had a slim chocolate ice cream bar that was easier to handle. It was culinary memory and muscle memory all at once. It also was a sweet memory of the small, simple, subtle ways my dad has always taken care of his family.

My dad has never been one of those overzealous fathers who jumps in the middle of everything. He was never a booster club member, but he was always there for the band concerts and the halftime shows. He was not a scoutmaster, but he didn't miss the courts of honor. What's more, he'd volunteer to pick up a load of us from summer camp and drive us home—with the windows down, enduring our reek from a week's worth of sweat and smoke.

Dad was the go-to guy when I procrastinated on a school project. I remember a Sunday afternoon when he typed out a research paper I had handwritten. He never edited or questioned my words; he just punched out what I had on his manual typewriter. He was a great typist, but he was a better writer. He composed a monthly letter and essay to his father and uncles and later to my brother and me. I learned from his words, and I didn't realize until later that I was also learning the discipline of writing—of doing it regularly. He also taught me the power of writing. His only published book, *Once There Were Three*, about the death of my sister, is still healing lives today.

Dad taught in unconventional ways. When we were kids, he'd spread a blanket on the ground at night and point out the constellations he learned as an Air Force navigator. Later, when I wanted to explore the cosmos myself, he let me spend my life savings of twenty dollars on model rockets.

A friend recently saw Dad at the car wash, cleaning up not his but my mother's car. He's always been good about that. He's a beast with a vacuum cleaner, too, and for better or worse, so am I.

Dad taught me the importance of dignity and privacy. In the sixth grade, when it was time to see the infamous films about reproduction, I was so embarrassed that I put the permission slip on Dad's dresser without saying a word. He signed it and put it back on my dresser without saying a word.

When my sister died and Dad's world fell apart, he kept his faith and kept the family going. When my world fell apart, his faith fed mine. He didn't try to make things better because he knew better than anyone that he couldn't do that. He knew the weight of loss, and his silent presence helped me carry my load.

When I moved to Dallas in 1983, Dad went with me to look for apartments and didn't raise any alarms when I chose one on the third floor. In fact, he helped me move my furniture. He was fifty at the time, and I'm pretty sure I wouldn't have done that for anyone when I was fifty.

When I was eager to get engaged the first time around, Dad quietly loaned me the cash to pay off the ring and acted like he'd forgotten about it when I repaid him months later. And even though I wandered off the Baptist farm and married a Catholic, he never said don't do it. He found plenty of common ground and stood firmly on it with me.

When I found love again, Dad cheered me on and welcomed LeAnn with open arms. And now he buys Fudgsicles by the box so there are plenty for everyone.

Family Histories

Every family has dates that loom large in its history. For the family I was born into it is June 16. That's the day my parents were married, and that's when the family officially started. But there's a double dip of family history because it is also my mother's birthday. Without her, there would have been no marriage, no children, no family at all.

But wait, there's more: A few weeks before my parents married, my father graduated from Baylor University and was commissioned into the U.S. Air Force, which meant that for the next three years the government would determine where this new couple would live and where their two sons would be born: my brother in Texas and me in Montana. Throw in the facts that my parents married on the day before Father's Day, and my brother was born a year and a day after that, and you can understand why I spend a lot of time in the greeting card aisle every year in early June.

Of course, there is some folklore woven into this family history. For instance, my parents only knew each other for a few months before becoming engaged. And my mother did not give my father a firm "yes" right away. And the story that my grandfather dropped to his knees in prayer when he learned of their engagement, distressed that his daughter would not finish college first. It all sounds rather shaky to me, but it doesn't change the outcome—that they created a loving relationship and family that have spanned the decades and withstood many tough tests.

Communities also have histories. Our neighborhood is marked with signs that state: "Embree: Est. 1886." The signs acknowledge that our neighborhood was the heart of what once was the Town of Embree, which was incorporated in 1886 and disincorporated in 1891 to become the new town of Garland.

One year our neighborhood association printed a walking tour guide that told not only that story but also highlighted some of the older homes on our streets. As with families, community histories contain ample portions of folklore, and a local historian took exception to some of the claims made by homeowners. He may be correct in some cases, but that doesn't change the bigger story: that we are the beneficiaries of the hard work and spirit of those who came before us and created the place we call home.

Our faith has a history, too, built on events and core beliefs and then overlaid with ideas that may be truth and may be folklore. While the fine details may lead to disagreements, the central story never changes: "Christ has died, Christ is risen, Christ will come again."

It's that story—more than our family tree or street address—that binds us together. If we keep this in focus, our future can outshine our history.

Bushels of Blessings

One of our favorite summertime excursions is to Ham Orchards about thirty miles east of Dallas on U.S. 80. We try to go there a couple of times every year, and a visit usually includes a barbecue sandwich under the tin-top pavilion, a stop inside the shop to buy peaches picked that morning from the orchard and produce from nearby farms including squash and watermelons, and then some homemade peach ice cream. A couple of times we've picked blackberries, but the peaches are the main draw, and the varieties change throughout the summer. It's a big operation with lots of friendly high school students working the counters, stocking the shelves, and carrying boxes of produce to cars.

One summer we stopped at Ham's as we left Dallas on a road trip to Louisiana. We would have stopped there again coming home, but we took a different route and had a very different experience. Just outside of Gilmer we passed a little produce stand in front of a house with a sign that read "Peaches," so we made a U-turn on the rural highway and went back. It was late on a Saturday afternoon, and we were surprised to find anyone there, but as we got out of the car we were greeted by an entire family: a couple who looked to be in their thirties, their two young children, and what was probably one of the couple's parents in their sixties.

Sitting on a table under a canopy were baskets of small but good-looking peaches. We eyed a half-bushel but settled for a quarter—enough to enjoy ourselves and to share with our parents and neighbors. As the sellers bagged them up, we got to talking and learned that this was a new family business. Just four years earlier they planted eight hundred peach trees on eight acres. They had a few peaches as the trees matured, but now they were harvesting and selling their first real crop.

As the younger couple told their story, I saw in their sunburned faces the fatigue from long days of work but also a glint of hope and expectation that the work would pay off. The children were shy and polite, with eyes that expressed wonder and a little bit of worry about their mom and dad's big dream. And in the eyes and smiles of the older parents I saw the sparkle of joy in the doing and faith in the knowing that pulling together as a family was going to be a success and was already delivering bushels of blessings.

Thinking about it later, I realized that about the same time that family was planting their peach trees, LeAnn and I were planting the seeds of a life together. While many of our friends have large Ham-sized marriages with bushels of children and grandchildren and baskets of memories and stories to tell, we started out late in life and we'll never be that big. We're more like that little family on the hillside outside of Gilmer. Our trees are new, but we've worked at it together, we've put everything we've got into it, trusted God with the soil and the weather, and we're giving thanks for abundant blessings.

Learning Me

"Are you two twins?" The man asking the question might have been kidding, but I bristled a little before I answered. "Sure, we're twins—born twenty-five years apart."

I was sitting beside my father in the waiting room at a physical therapist's practice, waiting on a session to work on a kink in his neck and back that's needed some attention. I accompanied Dad on the full series of appointments, and one day when he thanked me and apologized for the inconvenience, I said, "I'm glad to be here because I'm learning about myself." And truthfully, I was, because one thing the man who called us twins had right is that we share some traits: height, build, head shape, hairline, and, now, hair color. And with all those similarities lining up, I'm interested in what we share under the skin, especially skeletal frame and musculature, so I was more than happy to tag along and learn about myself.

Each of us is made from a mixture of genes that come from our fathers and our mothers, and each of their fathers and mothers, and on and on backward through time. The growing interest in genealogy is leading many people to DNA sampling to learn more about who they are and where they come from. I might do that someday, too, but with names such as Hampton, McIntire, McKenzie, and Wallace hanging in plain sight from the limbs of my family tree—and a fair complexion when I look in the mirror—it's a safe bet my roots are buried deep in the British Isles.

All of that knowledge about the past is fine but only if we use the information to positively impact who we are now and in the future. A family medical history is only useful if we pay attention to the tendencies and risks and adjust our lifestyle accordingly. Just listening to the physical therapist, I learned that I need to be more intentional about standing up straight, holding my head up, and sitting with my rear in the back of a chair instead of slouching. I already may have gained a half inch in height—or I may save myself an inch in compression in the coming years—just by following that simple advice.

Likewise, observing my parents over the years has taught me about the benefits of a lifestyle of physical exercise, healthy diet, continual learning, and mental exercise. Going deeper still, I've picked up on the importance of spiritual exercises such as praying, worshiping in community, and serving others. I've noticed with my parents and grandparents before them that even when the body begins to give in to wear and tear, exercising the soul can keep the spirit strong and ready for whatever may come.

Touchdowns and Wedding Vows

On a Saturday night we watched a football game we had recorded earlier in the day. We knew the outcome, and so there wasn't the usual tension and angst that come with not knowing if a good play will seal victory or if a fumble is a harbinger of defeat. We already knew that our team had won.

We missed the game because the youngest daughter of a lifelong friend was getting married. They are family and we wanted to be with them, so we were not disappointed by our decision. It was a beautiful service, a real family affair: the priest walked his mother down the aisle and then stood at the front to receive his sister on the arm of his father. Translation: the brother of the bride officiated. The wedding was followed by a cozy dinner with family and friends.

In his wedding homily, the brother of the bride commended the young couple for a faith and spiritual life that he said is "unusual for our generation," and he challenged them to love each other as Christ loves the church and as the church loves Christ.

They're just starting out and, based on what we know of their individual and joined faith stories, we have every expectation that their marriage will be great. They met at the brother's church, but long before that they were each nurtured in loving, faithful families. It looks like a marriage destined for the win column.

What we can't know ahead of time are the individual events that will mark their days and years. The joys and disappointments—the touchdowns and fumbles—can't be predicted. It won't be easy; I can guarantee that. The vows aren't for the easy, sunny days; the vows are for the stormy, heartbreaking days. The vows are for those moments when we feel like we've fallen too far behind to catch up and we're tired and bruised and don't think we can go on. That's why we recite the vows in church; that's why we ask the God who created marriage to join us in the marriage. That's also why the priest asks the friends and family to commit themselves to praying for the couple and cheering them on through whatever happens.

We've recorded football games before, but we rarely go back and watch them; we're satisfied if we've won, and too disheartened if we've lost. We were interested in this particular game because we weren't expecting to win, and it was something to have on the TV while we did other things. We like to have fun with it too: When something happens that causes the eventual losing team and their fans to celebrate, I'll say in an ominous voice, "People . . . I come from the future. Your joy is in vain. This will not end well." We can do the same thing when our team stumbles: "Don't despair; your struggles will be rewarded."

In televised football, that's a trick of technology to already know the ending while you're slogging through the first quarter. In marriage and life, knowing the ending is no trick; it's the result of hard work, faith, and commitment to vows. It helps to have fans cheering in the grandstand, too.

Basket Case

I spent the better part of a day and on into the wee hours of the morning shredding documents and throwing things away in preparation for moving and getting married. The clean-out was long overdue after nineteen years in the house. But like many people, I tend to hang on to things too long—even things that I've stopped using or really don't want to look at again. God's given us a good mind for memory, but we still want to keep physical proof of the journeys we've made.

I shredded bank statements, cancelled checks, credit card reports, telephone bills, and business receipts going back thirty years. I tried not to look at them, but I couldn't help but notice how little I was earning at the start of my career and how seemingly happy I was with so little. And I saw again the snowballing of debt over the years.

And then I pulled down from the closet shelf two square baskets. One held doctor bills and medical reports from the war with cancer that ended in defeat. I kept them in case some auditor came along insisting that something else was due, but I also think I kept them as proof to myself that we did everything we could do.

The other basket held hundreds of cards expressing prayers and support, and later, condolences. I kept the cards out of remembrance for those tender and emotional times, but also out of respect for all the kind people who had sent them. When someone writes such sweet and personal messages, you feel like you want to keep them forever. That's certainly what they insinuate on the greeting card commercials.

Looking at a few of the cards again, I realized that the same people who sent such lovely and touching messages had more recently been lifting me up with expressions of joy and anticipation: well wishes on the phone and by email, hugs and handshakes in the hallways at church, cards and gifts at showers, even an invitation to borrow a guest room and bath during the two weeks between the move and the wedding.

Any hesitation to hold on to the condolence cards was removed. It was clear what I had to do: empty the basket of sadness so it could hold all the joy I was receiving.

So, here's my question for you: What's in your basket?

Grumbling Samaritan

I missed a weekly meeting in order to take a friend home from the hospital. He was released a couple of days ahead of schedule and didn't have a ride, and I was his only option. When I emailed the others in the meeting that I would be absent and told them why, one emailed back, "Using the old Good Samaritan excuse, huh?"

I replied, "I'm grumbling as I go, and there's no Good Samaritan in that."

I was grumbling because it's a meeting I enjoy—a small group of writers who share their words and prod each other to keep working at it—and after the pickup and drop-off from the hospital, I would have to hustle to make another appointment that I wasn't going to enjoy so much.

But the writer responded again: "Hey, just showing up counts. You don't know how the Good Samaritan was feeling about rescuing that pesky guy on the side of the road."

I read the parable of the Good Samaritan again, and it's true: It says nothing about the Samaritan's attitude or demeanor in helping the man. It says the Samaritan bandaged his wounds, took him to an inn where he could rest and heal, left some money for ongoing care, and said he would be back to pay for anything else that was needed.

We assume he did all of that with a glad heart, but he might have hurried away in a huff because he was late to his next meeting. I'm programmed to think he was happy to help because of one of the first Bible verses I learned as a child, 2 Corinthians 9:7: "Each of you should give what you have decided in your heart to give, not reluctantly or under compulsion, for God loves a cheerful giver."

Actually, it was those last five words—"God loves a cheerful giver"—that were memorized and mostly in the context of giving an offering to the church. But I know now that the verse is about more than just money, because helping people is a gift that can be more valuable than money. And a gift given cheerfully? That's priceless.

If being a cheerful giver is what God loves, then I'm not so loveable. I grumble and mumble, moan and groan. When I see someone coming in search of a handout, my shoulders slump under the weight of what I feel is an imposition. I'm quick to give but slow to smile, and that probably taints the gift.

My friend hasn't said anything, but I'm sure the tone of my voice and my body language spoke loud and clear when I met him at the hospital. He was irritated about his hospital stay, and I was irritated by his irritation, and I'm sure I barked at a time when he needed some calming, soothing words. After all, he'd been in the hospital. It's not like he'd just come home from a cruise.

The parable of the Good Samaritan ends without us knowing if the Samaritan actually came back to check on the man. That's not the point of the story, but I'd like to think that he did as he promised and came back and provided help if it was needed. And I'd like to think that he was happy to help again.

My friend has needed to go back to the hospital for follow-up procedures, and I've taken him because I said I would. And each time I've tried to do more than just show up.

Connections

One Saturday we went to Weatherford, Texas, to hear my brother perform a concert. As he sang a pair of songs by gospel songwriter Stuart Hamblen, I looked over and saw LeAnn with tears in her eyes. As it turns out, the songs were among her father's favorites and ones that she often heard him sing while growing up.

When LeAnn and I first began getting to know each other, I learned that her father and mother met in Sherman, Texas, and her mother was raised in the tiny town of Whitewright nearby. My father grew up in Sherman, I lived there for a short while on the same street where LeAnn's aunt lived for many years, and my grandfather was raised in Whitewright.

LeAnn didn't know my late wife, Debra, but she has worked with people who knew her through religious education and publishing. LeAnn never worked with my mother, but as educators they have many close ties and connections in that community. That includes my mother's cousin Ginger, who rode with us to Weatherford and who is a speech pathologist by education just like LeAnn—as was my grandmother.

LeAnn and I didn't know each other at Baylor University, but there is a thick web of shared experiences that brings smiles and generates conversation. That was the case on that Saturday as we drove to Weatherford with my parents and cousins. The three couples were students at Baylor in different decades—the fifties, sixties and seventies—but we walked the same hallways and had some of the same professors.

I could go on and on with examples of these connections, but the point is that they are everywhere, and they are part of the connective tissue of our lives. We don't live alone, and if we look closely, we find that our paths crisscross and parallel each other in amazing ways.

I sometimes wonder if these connections are a foretaste of what heaven is like. I wonder who we will know and how we will know them. Will we be organized in family units, or will we be connected more generally through our mutual love of God? I tend to think that the people we rub shoulders with now—and the way we interact—will have meaning beyond this life.

A Box Full of Regrets

I got a box of books from Millie, an old friend from work. She didn't mail them to me or drop them off at my house because she doesn't know where I live. She didn't call or reach out on social media because we didn't have each other's numbers and she wasn't on social media. The sad truth is that we hadn't kept in touch very well since I left the job some years earlier.

But she knew where she could find me: at the church. She left the box with a receptionist, and I got a phone message that the box was waiting.

Inside I found six paperback reference books—the type that some writers used to keep close at hand: dictionaries of clichés, regional slang, colloquialisms, and anecdotes. Included with the books was a handwritten letter on yellow legal paper explaining that she was selling her small house "for more money than I ever dreamed," and with no family in Texas she was moving to Ohio to live near her sister and brother-in-law. They had retired as Baptist missionaries in Brazil after more than thirty years.

Millie and I worked in communications at the public transit agency; she did the internal work, and I did the external. We shared cubicle walls, a boss who was hard to work with, and a government agency culture that was painfully slow compared to our faster-paced journalistic training. We were mostly work colleagues, but we shared an occasional lunch where we talked about music, church, writing, and family. Millie was good to check on me when Debra was ill and later when I was grieving. Early during that time she coaxed me into a few outings to museums and the botanical garden just to get me out and about. She lived alone and knew what that was like.

The letter in the box opened with these words: "I have always admired you as a Christian, a husband, a journalist . . ." I'm pleased that perhaps my faith showed and that Millie knew my other "home" was the church. She came to some of our wind ensemble concerts and to mine and LeAnn's wedding. But I'm not pleased that my Christian witness didn't lead me to invite her to come on an ordinary Sunday, even though she was a regular at a Methodist church. And I'm not pleased that I didn't stay connected enough to invite her to my real home.

Millie closed her letter by saying, "I would appreciate it if you would keep me in your thoughts and prayers as I embark on this major milestone in my life."

I have done that, but I wanted to do more. I knew where she lived and tried to visit, but she was already gone. I mailed a note to her old address, hoping the postal service would forward it, and I included my return address. She hasn't replied, so I may never know if my note reached her.

I was hoping that maybe we could bridge the miles between Texas and Ohio better than we did across town in Dallas, but we seem to have failed at that. It's a hard lesson: friendships are only as good as you make them.

Feels Like Home

It was LeAnn's idea to celebrate my birthday by going to hear singer/songwriter Randy Newman in concert. She proposed it because she heard me mention once that I like Newman—especially his wonderfully crafted lyrics. That's one of LeAnn's many gifts:

She's always listening, always paying attention to what makes people smile, what fills us up, what lightens our load, what makes us feel at home.

I was hesitant at first. It would be expensive, it would be on a Sunday night, and we'd be out late after a busy day with work the next morning. She didn't push—LeAnn never pushes—but I said yes, and I'm so glad I did. It was a wonderful concert with just Newman, his piano, and his songs. We had great seats. We could hear well, and that's important because Newman has a difficult voice. And we were at just the right angle to see his hands moving across the keyboard and his feet tapping the floor. We leaned against each other as Newman treated us to his unique blend of satire and sentimentality. I'm so glad I said yes.

I'm even more glad that I said "yes" some years ago when LeAnn suggested we have a birthday dinner together. Again, she was paying attention. She had learned (perhaps I told her) that my fiftieth birthday was approaching. Her birthday is just four days before mine, so she said that we should celebrate together. I was a fairly new widower, and while I had already agreed to a quiet dinner with my parents and a few friends, there was grief in my heart and an empty place at the table. I wasn't feeling much like celebrating.

Still, I said yes to LeAnn's suggestion, not knowing what would begin that night for both of us. A good meal and slow service caused us to sit and talk much longer than we might have otherwise. We both left the restaurant feeling like we'd had a nice time—perhaps starting a new friendship—but neither of us expected anything more.

Over the next two years friendship grew slowly and steadily, season after season, until love was planted in us. And now each year when we come around to our shared birthdays, we find that we share so much more. It turns out God is paying attention, too, knowing what makes us smile, what fills us up, what lightens our load, what makes us feel at home.

The high point of the concert for us both came at the very end—a lovely song called "Feels Like Home," with the lines:

If you knew
How much this moment
Means to me
And how long I've waited for your touch
If you knew
How happy you are making me
I never thought I'd love anyone so much
Feels like home to me
Feels like home to me

Feels like I'm all the way back where I come from
Feels like home to me
Feels like home to me
Feels like I'm all the way back where I belong.[2]

There's no gift that LeAnn and I can give each other that will ever equal what God has given us both: a love to share, a feeling of home.

Set in Stone

When LeAnn and I celebrated our first anniversary, we ignored the traditional route of paper gifts and gave each other stone: two tons of charcoal flagstone and three yards of decomposed black granite. The gift charts say that paper is the gift for the first year and you have to wait ninety years to get to stone. With life expectancies what they are—and us not getting married until we were in our fifties—we decided we better not wait to get to the heavy stuff.

The stone was for the walkway leading to our front door. Our neighborhood has extremely deep parkways (that strip of lawn between the sidewalk and the street). They are twelve feet, and when it came time to pave our sidewalks and driveway, we decided that we didn't want more concrete crossing the parkway, so we opted for flagstone. While we had plenty of offers from landscapers to do the work, we decided to do it ourselves. We wanted to save money, and on top of that, we thought it'd be a good project to do together.

We might have had an easy start of it because our landscaper put in grass everywhere except in that location, but time passed, and the weeds came in, and we spent the better part of three mornings digging out the area. On the third morning, we went to the local stone yard and bought the flagstone and decomposed granite. Amazingly, the vendor delivered it that afternoon.

The next morning, a Saturday, we spread the decomposed granite about two inches deep and picked through the pallet of flagstone looking for pieces that would fit just right. Some we could handle individually, but many we had to carry and set down together. While the digging of the previous week was drudgery, laying the stone was fun—like putting together a big puzzle as we looked for pieces that would fill out the space and interlock with each other to some extent.

We rested on Sunday, and then on Monday morning, we leveled the stones—with me lifting the corners and LeAnn shoveling in small loads of granite. When we had it looking as level as we could, we dumped more granite into the seams and then swept it around until the gaps were filled. With rain in the forecast, we were expecting the granite and stone to shift a little and even sink down, but we had enough decomposed granite left over to make adjustments. We also had enough granite and stone to create a walkway down the side of our house and to start a similar project on our back patio.

I'd be leaving out a big part of the story if I didn't mention the help we got in this endeavor. On the first morning, a neighbor came, unannounced and uninvited, with a shovel and helped dig out the area. She came again the second morning with her shovel and also some stakes and yellow cord to help mark the level. For the record, I was going to do the same thing myself, but she beat me to it. On the third morning of digging, she came again, and we were joined by LeAnn's father, who we invited to help dig and to go with us to buy the stone and granite. We also had plenty of people walk by and drive by with vocal support if not actual help. When we got to the stone selecting and laying, we were left to ourselves. I'm glad for that, because that was the personal, subjective, aesthetic phase of the project, and it really was up to LeAnn and me to work it out.

And that's the way it is with marriage. There can be some help and support as things are planned and developing, but the final design and success of the relationship is up to the two people who have joined their lives together. People still can offer advice, but it's up to the couple to do the heavy lifting needed to make it work—whether in the first year of paper, or in the ninetieth year of stone.

Journeys

When LeAnn and I were planning our honeymoon, we set a few goals. We wanted a few days alone to rest and relax after the months of planning the wedding and the event itself, but we also needed some flexibility because we were selling two houses and might need to get home fast. So, we planned a road trip down through the middle of Texas and back. We planned the first two days in advance, but after that we left things to chance and whim. We had a general list of places we might want to go and things we might want to see, but we decided to go where the traveling muses led us—and the realtors back home allowed.

In some ways this loosely planned trip was like life itself. You can do some planning in advance, set some goals, makes some assumptions about the future, but at some point you have to be flexible and leave things to fate—or better yet, faith.

I've not yet met an adult of a certain age who can say their life has played out exactly the way they planned or hoped. They were traveling along just fine, but then something happened to knock them off course: they lost a job or a loved one; health issues threatened their lives and their resources; relationships changed; the storms of life blew away their dreams and aspirations. Good things can happen too that nonetheless change the direction we are headed: an unexpected love, an unexpected child, an exciting career opportunity, a transfer to a new city.

Some people say that God is present in every detail, and I believe that many times this is true. I also believe that sometimes life just happens, but even then God is there to help lead us in a new direction. And I believe that God is full of surprises if we're open to them.

A couple of years before LeAnn and I married, a good friend saw me at a Holy Week service and leaned across the pew to declare, "Easter always comes just in time." I didn't ask him what he meant, but what I got from those words was that God's grace always arrives just when we need it. The friend knew that LeAnn and I were beginning to spend time together, and his words hinted that God was leading us on a new journey together.

Gladly, the journey continues.

Careless Living

Careless living: that's how LeAnn and I jokingly explain how we got to where we are today. It all started innocently with a casual dinner between a widower and a single woman to mark each other's same-week birthdays. But then we got careless and started spending time together, which led to dating, engagement, marriage, selling two houses, and building a new home together.

It was actually intentional carelessness, as in not overthinking everything, not trying to control things, not worrying about the outcome but instead just going along and trusting our lives and our hearts to God. Had we been more careful and controlling, it's doubtful we would have gotten to this place.

You see, I wasn't looking to get married again. If life had gone a different way, I'd be celebrating thirty-five-plus years of marriage with Debra. That changed, and if I had followed the new script that I thought I'd been given, I'd be counting the years I'd lived alone. There'd have been nothing wrong with that. Similarly, if LeAnn had stuck to what she thought was the script for her life, she'd have been on her own today too. But by carelessly throwing away all the scripts and expectations and trusting God, we started a new chapter of a story of faith, hope, and love together.

On a similar note: On the Saturday evening before we moved into the new house we built together, we placed a birdbath and bird feeder in our new backyard and sat on the porch to watch the birds. The few that came hopped around in the grass but apparently were too busy looking for food on the ground to notice the banquet right above their heads. By the next day the birds had discovered the feeder, and they've been feasting ever since. All they had to do was quit trying so hard and look up.

Sometimes that's all we need to do.

If I Could Say It Over Again

"Are you okay?" In the split-second after I asked that I wanted to take it back because I knew it was insanely stupid. The friend I was speaking to was grieving the loss of his wife, and his answer was honest and expected: "No, I'm not okay."

Of all people, I should have known better, but it was a reflex response to seeing someone in distress. What I meant was: "Is there something I can do at this precise moment to help you in any way?" but that would have been a ridiculous question too, because there was nothing I could do short of bringing his wife back that would be any help. All I could do—all any of us can do—is be there and let the person know they are not alone. And if possible, when the time is right, we might say something or do something that makes sense.

Take, for example, the advice I received a couple of months after my first wife died. I was trying to track down some of her long-ago friends and let them know what had happened. One of them, Kathy, a social worker and minister, emailed her condolences and then said, "Grieve well." I wish I had kept the email, but I can paraphrase the rest of what she said: Experience your grief fully so that God can work through you and with you to memorialize her appropriately but also to draw meaning, consolation, and faith in your own life from the entire experience.

I can't say that I followed that advice explicitly, but I don't think it is something that a person can really work at. Rather, it is something that you have to let happen to you; you have to open yourself to what God will do.

A few years later at a class reunion I saw Kathy for the first time since our email conversation. I thanked her once more for her advice, and then I introduced her to LeAnn. "God has been good," I said. And then just forty hours later, I asked the stupid question, "Are you okay?" So now, I'd like to pass Kathy's advice on to my friend and add my own testimony that some day—in God's good time, and in God's good way—you will be okay.

Treasures Old and New

In our Bible study class at church, we looked at some of Jesus' parables, specifically the ones in the Gospel of Matthew that describe the kingdom of heaven. We ended with this one from Matthew 13: "He said to them, 'Therefore every teacher of the law who has become a disciple in the kingdom of heaven is like the owner of a house who brings out of his storeroom new treasures as well as old'" (v. 52).

Among our discussion points was the idea that this was not about "out with the old and in with the new," but about bringing the best of both old and new into play. After all, Jesus said earlier in Matthew, "Do not think that I have come to abolish the Law or the Prophets; I have not come to abolish them but to fulfill them" (5:17).

The idea of bringing together old and new treasures resonated with me because LeAnn and I were coming up on the anniversary of the day some years earlier when we merged our lives and all of our worldly possessions in the house we built together. That included old things we each brought to our marriage and some new things we'd accumulated, including some wedding gifts.

We could have arranged all those items ourselves, but we thought it would be interesting and actually smart to let a neutral party have a go at it. We already had contacted Barbara, a church friend and decorator, to help us decide where to put our mix of his and hers furniture. That was important to decide before our move-in day because we were paying the movers by the hour. But the more delicate and potentially sensitive task was taking all of our decorative pieces, knickknacks, and mementos and deciding where they should go. Many of those items represented pieces of our personal stories that had been decades in the writing before we had turned a new page together.

So we emptied boxes of stuff out on tables and countertops and even the floor and watched as Barbara gently picked up each item, examined it, looked around the rooms and chose a perfect place for it. She didn't know what belonged to me or to LeAnn. She placed items where they would make the best statement about our new home and our life together.

Looking around our rooms today, everything is exactly where it should be. What's more, I can't recall the origins of some items. Was it mine? Was it hers? Is it old? Is it new? I don't know. I've come to believe that God has gifted me with a cloudy memory—or a healthy ambivalence—about trinkets and treasures. This blurring of the past has helped me embrace today and tomorrow. And the blending of old and new has helped create a new way of living.

Leaving the Island

"No man is an island." That was the subject of an email from a dear friend on a Friday morning, and the irony couldn't have been greater because at that moment I was mopping up water from a washing machine leak that had covered our new utility room floor and had oozed onto the hardwood in the kitchen.

Beyond the visual irony of me standing in a pool of water, the email was about generosity, and I was fighting the demon that most keeps me from being generous: obsessive cleanliness. I've always liked to keep things neat and clean, fresh and new, and that's been a deterrent to so many good and enjoyable things. I've never gotten into cooking because you can't cook and be neat at the same time. My Bible doesn't have scribbles in the margins. My blankets don't have grass stains where I dragged them out onto the lawn to lie on and look at the stars like we did as kids. My car doesn't have food crumbs and stains on the seats that say, "We've been on a rollicking carefree road trip." The list goes on.

But most of all, this obsession has prevented me from being a good host, or at least a comfortable host. You can't be hospitable and obsessive at the same time. Caring too much about the condition of your stuff stands in the way of sharing your stuff with others. To be truly generous in sharing something, you have to invite someone to enjoy it—not the way you enjoy it or the way you want them to enjoy it, but the way they would enjoy it if it was truly theirs. To be generous and hospitable is not to say, "Come in and have a cup of coffee but only if you sit at my table and don't spill it," but rather to say, "Come in and grab a cup and sit back on the sofa and put your feet up if you wish."

That goes for a house. It also goes for our other possessions, our church, our faith, our love. To be truly generous is to say, "What's mine is yours without limitations or parameters." And, as the friend said in her email, "Generosity requires relationship—the giver to the receiver." You can't hold back.

I was discussing this with my brother later that evening as I helped him unload his car. He and his wife and two young sons were our first overnight guests in the new house, and I confessed that the morning flood and now the family visit was going to be a good test for me because I hate being so protective of things. He told me that he tried to keep their new house in perfect condition when they first moved in some years ago, but with five boys and lots of houseguests, it was futile. Besides, he said, he couldn't be a good host and worry about that.

And then he reminded me of the first time we visited his house and he offered us their master bedroom, which we accepted and enjoyed. He said, "You know, I can still see the wheel marks on the floors from the luggage that you rolled into our bedroom." I cringed at the damage we had caused and that he had never mentioned until then, but he just smiled at the memory of the visit that is engraved in his floor.

He Is Risen; She Is Too

There was no sunny joy on Easter Sunday, 1971. Instead of going to my grand-parents' church and then hunting Easter eggs under the East Texas pines, we were at our home church for the first time that I could remember. A car wreck on the road to our annual Easter celebration had ended my sister Martha's life and changed our lives forever.

As we sat in church that Sunday morning, the congregation around us celebrated Christ's resurrection and the promise of eternal life. I'm sure that someone said to me, "She's alive with Jesus, and that's the joy of Easter." At age twelve I knew that was the center of our faith, but I felt cheated. While the tomb in Jerusalem was empty, the grave at the cemetery was full.

From my perspective, we couldn't have been farther away from Martha on that resurrection day, but the miracle of Easter is that she was and is as close as a breath of air. Like the disciples, I needed help understanding that. For them, it came at Pentecost. As Jesus promised them in the Gospel of John, "The Holy Spirit, whom the Father will send in my name, will teach you all things and will remind you of everything I have said to you" (14:26).

For me, that truth didn't come in a mighty wind or in tongues of fire but in the gentle love of those around me. In that regard, being "the hands and feet of Christ" is not just a neat idea; it is very real and should be taken seriously.

And the truth came in simple moments that helped point the way for the future. On that Monday after Easter when I went back to school, a fellow sixth grader named Ricky walked up to my desk, said, "I'm sorry," and then sat down. Class began as usual and I knew that while life was changed, it wasn't over.

Indeed, that was decades ago and there's been plenty of living. In those years I haven't been to the cemetery more than a dozen times. I know that the grave is as empty as the tomb in Jerusalem. I don't have physical proof of that—that's why we call it "faith"—but I know that Martha's spirit lives because I've felt the Holy Spirit inside of me, and I've seen it at work through you.

NEIGHBORS:
NEXT DOOR AND DOWN THE STREET

As best I can figure, I've lived at fifteen distinct addresses, which means I've lived in fifteen neighborhoods—some for just a year, the longest for nineteen. How I've lived in those neighborhoods has spanned the full range of experiences. I've been a spectator and an organizer, a joiner and a hermit, a reliable friend and a quiet crank.

Of all the communities of which we are members, our neighborhoods afford us the most leeway. We can choose our neighbors for the most part, and when we can't, we can choose how much and in what ways we connect with them. We can close our doors and turn our backs, or we can engage and try to create something special.

Signs of a Good Neighborhood

Three months before LeAnn and I married, we had dinner on the grounds. That is, we had a picnic on the lot where we planned to build a house together.

We probably were an odd sight, but most of the people who drove by smiled and waved. I think that's a good sign of a friendly neighborhood. I told LeAnn it would be a bad sign if boys on bicycles with BB guns came and chased us away. That might have been a sign of an overactive imagination, because I don't think boys with BB guns roam neighborhoods as they did when I was growing up.

As we munched on chicken, salad, and fruit—what else on a picnic?—we counted and identified the trees around the perimeter and watched as robins, mockingbirds, and doves danced around the yard and trees. We noticed that the coos of doves seemed to come from every direction, and that's a sign of a good neighborhood too.

And then we imagined where we might be sitting in the house some day when it was finished. We didn't have a final plan yet, but we'd looked at dozens and we knew where we wanted things to be. It was a big corner lot, so we wanted a long porch across the front and running down the side. We wanted lots of open space for entertaining on the first floor, a big kitchen with a big pantry and windows over the sink looking out on a garden, and a master suite on the first floor so we won't have to climb the stairs when we're old. Upstairs, we wanted more bedrooms for visiting family and friends and an office for us both. And we wanted windows—lots of windows everywhere. That's a sign of a good house.

After we ate, we packed up our dinner and then walked the lot and picked up some stray trash. We didn't live there yet, but we were already trying to be good neighbors. It was, after all, going to be a good house in a good neighborhood.

Ready for Guests

While building our house, LeAnn and I lived in an apartment nearby. We reached a major turning point when we finally had doors to lock; that didn't mean we were ready to move in yet—it was an acknowledgment that this was, in fact, a private home and would soon have permanent residents.

Until we had doors, the house was open to the world, and we knew that we'd had lots of people walking through. One Saturday we were there to check on things and a man walked in to look around. After we got over being startled by each other, we introduced ourselves as the owners, and he said he was just curious because he had done a lot of renovations himself. He was amiable and courteous, so we gave him a quick tour. We happily did the same thing over the months with friends, family, and future neighbors. One day a neighbor stopped by with a small dog in her arms, and at her request I gave her and the pup a tour.

I've done my share of walking into houses that are under construction. If the house was framed but there wasn't a door, I'd walk in to look around. The only time I ever walked into a house that was further along was when I was in the third grade. One day after school I rode my bike to a street where new houses were being built. I walked in the front door of one of the homes and down the hall where I was stopped by a man working in the bathroom. "Hey, you can't be in here. There's gonna be people living here soon," he said. I answered, "I know, and I'm one of them." It was going to be our house in a few weeks, and I was checking out my new bedroom.

Aside from that one occasion, if there is a door on the structure, then I always wait for an invitation, including the ones on signs that say, "Open House" or "Estate Sale." I remember a time while I was growing up when my parents would make the rounds of open houses on Saturday and Sunday afternoons. They were just looking around, getting ideas, and even I liked taking a peek at the kinds of places other people lived, especially if there were stairs because we always lived in one-story houses. My interest in open houses was dampened, however, after I took a tumble down some stairs on a late Sunday afternoon.

Another incident ended my interest in estate sales. I shopped a lot of those sales when I was younger and accumulating stuff, and one day I walked through the open door of a house that had an estate sale sign in the yard. The house was mostly empty until I walked into a back room where a woman was sitting in a chair watching TV. "What the hell are you doing in my house?" she shouted, and I answered, "I thought there was an estate sale." She said, "That was last week." I apologized and quickly left, closing the front door on the way out. I should have taken down her sign, too.

So as soon as we had doors on our new house, we began locking them and double-checking them before we left after each visit. But that doesn't mean we weren't planning to be neighborly. We designed the house with room to entertain and vowed to host events and encourage spur-of-the-moment visits. That's the kind of home we wanted then and have now. If you let us know you're coming, we might even put out some cookies and iced tea. After all, LeAnn loves to cook and she has the spiritual gift of hospitality. Me? I have plenty of patience . . . and lots of good attic space where I can disappear when I get tired.

Walking and Talking Together

I made Edna cry. I didn't mean to, but I did. I was standing on the sidewalk, hand-watering the dead, weedy lawn, when from behind me I heard a voice: "Trying to save your yard?"

I turned and it was Edna, one of the first people we met when we moved into the neighborhood. She caught our attention early because she would walk by almost every day with her dog—not on a leash tugging her along but tucked up under her arm. And this wasn't a little purse dog or a miniature; it was black and white and shaggy and about the size of a large watermelon. I asked Edna about this once and she said her dog had trouble walking, so she did the walking for both of them.

We hadn't seen Edna in a while, so when I saw her this time I was pleased. But I noticed immediately that her arms were empty, and embarrassed that I couldn't remember the pup's name, I asked, "Where's your little dog today?"

She swallowed hard and in a soft voice said, "He passed away a week ago on Friday."

"I'm so sorry," I said, and she said, "I really miss him. I miss my husband too." And then her lips trembled, and her eyes watered, and she turned her head away and walked down the sidewalk.

"I'm sorry to have upset you," I called after her but there was no reply.

And indeed, I was sorry to have upset her, but maybe I didn't do the upsetting. Maybe it was life that upset her, and maybe I just brought it to the surface. And maybe she needed to share that upset with someone because she lives alone now and has no one to talk to except perhaps people like me who she meets on the street.

We're taught by society to strive for success and joy and all the good things in life, but when the big troubles come, we don't know what to do about them. Sometimes our family and friends don't know what to do about them either, so they keep a distance or even go away.

Having walked in Edna's shoes—grieving a pet, mourning a spouse—I know how important it is to share those hurts. When my losses were still fresh, I was sometimes desperate to have someone ask something or say something so that I could release a little pressure and perhaps put words to a sweet memory. But most everyone else was ready to move on, or they thought that talking would upset me, so there was usually silence.

But I'm here to tell you: It can be awkward to ask people in pain how they are doing, and it may bring up emotions and it may get messy. And you can even stumble into it like I did with Edna and send someone walking away with tears running down their cheeks. But the danger is not in asking; the danger is in not caring enough to ask.

A Difficult Day in the Neighborhood

"Hey . . . HEY . . . you know it's against federal law to put something other than mail in a mailbox."

I walked back one house and stood face-to-face with the man who shouted at me and stood quietly as he repeated that statement. I reached forward, took the crumpled piece of paper out of his hand, and calmly said, "I'm sorry. We won't bother you ever again." I leaned hard on that word "ever" and stopped short of saying what I felt: "We don't want your type anyway."

That was the one little hiccup in my effort one evening to distribute flyers inviting neighbors to our National Night Out block party. I shouldn't have been surprised, though. Two years earlier when we distributed flyers announcing our new neighborhood association, I received an email from someone regarding mailbox abuse. Now I was meeting him face to face. He's probably about my age, my size, with a shaved head that seems to intensify his wrinkled brow and angry frown.

By the way, I looked it up and technically he is right about his mailbox. I only tried to use it because there was no place else to put the flyer: no chair, no flowerpot, and certainly no welcome mat. The house is neat but with no landscaping—perhaps because yard work means he might have to spend time outside and engage someone such as me.

Just three houses earlier I had met for the first time a newcomer to the neighborhood. He was out watching a sprinkler he had placed on a bare spot under a tree. He looked at the flyer and asked if it would be okay if he cooked hot dogs for everyone. "That'd be great," I said, and then he told me about some of the work he'd done on the house. He was freely offering details about himself that I hadn't asked for. "Just the type we do want," I thought.

The contrast couldn't have been greater, and it was easy to make a quick judgment about the angry man—that some people are just mean and angry by nature. They don't want to be a part of anything. They want to be left alone and so that's exactly what we should do. We'll not only leave them alone; we'll ignore them completely. As far as we're concerned, their house is empty.

But not so fast: No one comes out of the womb that way. Most likely there's a backstory to this man's anger. I may never know it, and it isn't my right to know it, but it just may be my responsibility as a neighbor to respect it and make room for it—and certainly not to judge it.

After all, I lived in my previous neighborhood for nineteen years, and while I provided financial and moral support to the neighborhood association, I did so from behind closed doors. I didn't go to any events or meetings. I didn't want to be bothered. I wanted to be left alone. No wonder that when death changed my world and I found myself living alone, no one from the neighborhood came calling. They gave me what I had wanted: total privacy. I reaped exactly what I had sown.

It's strange now that I'm the one roaming the neighborhood handing out flyers, and stranger yet that I agreed to be president of our neighborhood association when we formed it. And once again, I'm reaping what I'm sowing. During the summer when we were out of town and got a call from our security company, I called a neighbor. As soon as I said "alarm" he interrupted and said, "I'm walking to your house right now," and we stayed on the phone as he checked every door and window. A false alarm brought an example of the blessing that comes when we are neighborly to our neighbors.

So, what should I do about the angry man on the block? The first thing is to set aside the response I dreamed up in my childish imagination: to sneak over there at night and superglue his mailbox shut once and for all. That would show him, right? Wrong. That would just show him the mean person I can be in my mind, and by association, what kind of mean neighborhood association we are, which we aren't at all. We're a friendly, live-and-let-live neighborhood, and I'll try to respond in that manner.

Bottom line: Our neighbors don't have to come to the party to be our neighbors. They don't have to be friendly or nice or helpful or anything at all. They are our neighbors because they share the street with us. But it's a two-way street, and regardless of how they choose to travel it, we have a choice in how we travel it too: angry, friendly, indifferent, respectful, closed, open. The choices are many.

Standing Down, Standing By

"I want them gone." With those four words, the battle ended before it started, and the warriors stood down.

I'm talking about what happened in our neighborhood when someone sounded the alarm that the city was going to cut down two mature trees—a beautiful cedar and an oak—to make way for a sidewalk where there wasn't one. We have a neighborhood association and while we don't have and don't want any legal jurisdiction, we certainly are ready to rise to the occasion when a neighbor's property is threatened. So as president of the association, I jumped on our website and announced we were ready to do whatever we could to protect the trees and work with the city on an alternative plan for the sidewalk. I even suggested that we would rally around the trees if the chain saws came before we worked something out.

And then LeAnn and I drove down the street and around the corner to survey the battleground. When we saw the homeowner sitting outside, we lowered the car window and I said, "We're going to work with you to save those trees." And that's when he walked up to the car window and said, "I don't want the trees. I want them gone."

Wow, we did not see that coming! We sat in silence a moment and then listened as he explained. His reasoning was straightforward and sensible: the trees were on the city easement, and yet he was responsible for both their upkeep and any damage they might do if they fell. He preferred that the city pave the easement with a sidewalk. In fact, he said he'd been working with the city on that for several months. "I want them gone."

There was nothing else to say but, "Oh . . . okay. It's your property and if that's what you want, then we'll not do anything else."

Personally, I still hated to see the trees go. If it were my property, I'd welcome the beauty and the shade that the tall trees provide. I'd protect them with occasional trimming, and I'd make sure my homeowner's insurance covered damage should they fall. But it's not my property, and I can't tell someone else what to do with their property. If they'd rather have the trees gone, then that's their right and I respect that.

Sometimes the people we want so badly to help don't need or want our help, and there's nothing we can do. We can only stand by, let them make their decision, and respect their right to own their decision. But we also might stay close because we might see a chance to help in a different way.

If we hadn't driven by and checked on things, we would have missed hearing the truth about what is actually going on. And who knows, perhaps if we drive by more often, we might see an opportunity to be a good neighbor.

The homeowner replaced the cedar and oak with trees of his own choosing up on his lawn where he really wanted them. Just like us, he still likes trees.

Making Connections

LeAnn and I couldn't help but smirk at each other as we went back over the series of unexpected connections we'd just made. And we couldn't help but think that God was in the details.

It started forty-eight hours earlier, when a phone call told us that the house we wanted to sell would be shown from three to five on Sunday afternoon. As we cleaned and tidied things up, we planned our exile: run some errands, check out the sale at a bookstore, and perhaps look at the new apartments in downtown Garland. When the house sold, we would need a place to live until the new house was built.

After taking care of the errands, we decided to skip the bookstore and go to the apartments. We toured a model, and as we were leaving the leasing center another potential tenant came in, saw us, and said, "LeAnn?!" Quick introductions revealed that the woman, Carol, is an acquaintance of LeAnn and a downtown resident with a house that a mutual friend encouraged us months earlier to look at for ideas. We mentioned it, and Carol said, "I've been wanting to show you my house." Within minutes we were at her house looking around.

In the midst of talking about home building, we explained that our vacant lot had to be replatted with a vote from the planning commission set to meet on Monday night. Carol said, "You probably know Louis on the commission because he went to Baylor just like you did."

Incredulous, I said, "You mean the Louis who was the religion writer for the *Houston Chronicle* at the same time I was covering religion at the Waco newspaper?" And she said, "Yes." I hadn't seen Louis since our career paths had crossed almost thirty years earlier, but I knew him by reputation.

So, the next night we went to the planning commission meeting with Steve, our builder, and sure enough there was Louis sitting with the other commissioners. They were having a pre-meeting conference, and Louis asked city staff why our property was being replatted. They explained their process, and when it came time for a vote, it was approved unanimously. We didn't have to stand up and explain or defend anything.

After the meeting, LeAnn, Steve, and I went down front to introduce ourselves to Louis. I made the "former religion writer" connection with him, and then more conversation led to more connections, including the fact that we were all Baylor grads, and Louis and Steve were fraternity brothers. We walked out together talking about downtown Garland (where Louis and his wife also lived) and our common dreams for the neighborhood. We left city hall feeling that perhaps we had an advocate for our little part of helping revitalize old downtown Garland. We also left with mutual promises to stay in touch and get together as new neighbors—which we have done.

We also left feeling God's presence in bringing us to an intersection of people and places where exciting things are possible. Without question, God is asking, "What will you do with this now?" The answer is up to us.

One of *Those* Houses

One Sunday night as I was going to bed, I looked out the front windows and was provoked by what I saw: It was raining and our sprinklers were on. "We're not one of *those* houses," I grumbled as I rushed out to the garage to turn the system off.

We've all seen those houses, and I've been the first one to shake my head and wag a finger and even mutter "wasteful idiot" under my breath. But I am not a wasteful idiot because I know why the sprinklers came on.

The night before I had stopped the sprinklers from coming on at their usual time in deference to our neighbors, who had a crowd of people at their house with cars parked along our curb. I sighed under the feeling of invasion, but I knew that we had been one of those houses often enough. We've had church groups, family reunions, and office friends over who have parked up and down the street. And I thought about how messy it would be for these people to come out to their cars and have to jump through the sprinklers, so I reset the system for midnight, but I botched the programming in the process.

On Sunday, we had our parents over for Mother's Day lunch and the neighbors were at it again, with a dozen cars parked around. We figured it must be an extended Mother's Day gathering, but after we walked LeAnn's parents out to their car and watched them drive away, we learned the truth. A man about our age walked toward us, apologized for all the cars, and said, "My mother-in-law passed yesterday."

We were shocked to learn that Julie had been ill with pancreatic cancer for five years—the entire time we had lived next door. We had introduced ourselves when we moved in and waved whenever we saw her, which was often. We told the son-in-law how Carl, Julie's husband, leaves every morning at eight thirty to work on remodeling projects, and Julie usually left a little bit later. He said, yes, she kept living a full life despite a poor prognosis. He told us that we might have seen them all outside with balloons some months earlier, and we had. He explained that was the fourth anniversary since Julie's diagnosis; it was a celebration of life. But then he told us that she had taken a turn for the worse, and we realized we hadn't seen her in weeks. It's amazing what you can see and yet not see or not understand, especially with people who live quietly and privately.

I was one of those houses once upon a time. If the neighbors had been watching, they'd have seen people coming with food after a surgery, slow walks around the block during recovery, our coming and going as usual as if we had the disease under control, and then parents' cars parked out front for days when things got bad. They might have noticed a quieting of movement, and then at sunrise on a July morning they'd have seen the van from the funeral home and then a fresh wave of cars parked along the curb.

The cars were lined up again on Monday. LeAnn baked some beans and ham, and we took them over just as some of the group was mingling outside. They received our offerings with hugs and handshakes and apologized again for all the cars. "Anytime," we said.

Because we've all been or will be one of those houses at one time or another—the one that hosts the parties and reunions, the recovering and surviving, the mourning and grieving. And sometimes the sprinklers will come on while it's raining.

A Year of Eternity

It was cloudy, chilly, and damp; it was sunny, warm, and dry. We heard laughter and fond greetings; we saw tears and consoling hugs. There was sadness for lives lost and broken; gratitude for the binding of community. There were words of civic pride and hymns of reverent comfort.

Such was the range of sights, sounds, and emotions on the shore of Lake Ray Hubbard as citizens of Garland marked the anniversary of the night of December 26, 2015, when an EF4 tornado dropped down out of the sky. Nine people were killed on Interstate 30, thousands of homes were damaged or destroyed, and untold numbers of lives were shattered.

It was hard to believe a year had passed. For most of us, the year had gone by breathlessly fast, as most years do, but for those whose lives were overturned, it may have been painfully slow. The year had brought relief in the form of homes repaired or rebuilt, businesses refurbished and reopened. But those who lost loved ones will never see restoration. Their lives are forever changed. And although the passing days may bring comfort, life will never be as it was.

The remembrance event at the lake was a snapshot of what we all experience—if not in a year's time then over a lifetime. There will be cold rain and warm sunshine, tears and laughter, sadness and gratitude. In fact, as we listened and watched, I recalled Ecclesiastes 3, which begins with the familiar words, "There is a time for everything, and a season for every activity under the heavens" (v. 1). What follows is a long list that I've heard read in Sunday morning sermons and at weddings and funerals. It begins with "a time to be born and a time to die, a time to plant and a time to uproot," and ends with "a time to love and a time to hate, a time for war and a time for peace" (vv. 2, 8).

And then follows these words that I so often overlook: "What do workers gain from their toil? I have seen the burden God has laid on the human race. He has made everything beautiful in its time. He has also set eternity in the human heart; yet no one can fathom what God has done from beginning to end" (vv. 9-11).

Translations vary but it's a remarkable juxtaposition of ideas. A quick-read interpretation might be: Our burdens are God-given and are ultimately beautiful when looked at through the prism of eternity. I don't know if that was the writer's intended message, but I find myself holding tightly to the idea that God has a plan—it's called eternity—and there's no way to understand it.

Likewise, I've grown into the idea that we are already living in eternity and that events such as what happened a year earlier in our community are markers on a continuum with no beginning or end. That is how I have been able to endure my own losses and appreciate the joy and rebirth that have followed.

That may be little comfort now for those who lost so much to the tornado. To them, time may have felt like an eternity without relief. But just as the clouds gave way to sunshine on the day of remembrance, there is hope that God will make all things beautiful in time.

Coffee and Conversation

It's happened before and it happened again: I was mowing the lawn and noticed movement out of the corner of my eye. I turned to see our neighbor coming across the street, elbows raised high, with a small white cup and saucer in his hands. It was time for coffee and conversation.

I suppressed a grumble that expressed my thoughts of "I really need to get the yard mowed before it starts raining," and I swallowed back my discomfort about the fact that my neighbor doesn't speak English and I don't speak Spanish. That apparently doesn't bother him because he's the one who always comes across the street. He's the brave one; he's the one with the gift of hospitality.

So, we stood on the sidewalk, me sipping the cup of potent espresso from his native Cuba, and him watching and smiling. Uncomfortable with the silence, I paused between sips—you don't gulp café Cubano—and asked, "Como se dice?" ("How do you say?") and pointed to something and he nodded and gave me the Spanish word. I nodded back and gave him the English word. I'd like to think we are both learning a little, except that I don't have a good memory for the words he's given me for grass, lawn mower, sky, rain, heat, sidewalk, work. I do remember "gracias" as I hand him the empty cup.

We've done this several times, and we'll probably do it again. In between these one-on-one moments of coffee and conversation we wave from across the street.

Sometimes I say, "Hola," and he replies with "Howdy," but often the greeting is silent.

It's not unlike the conversations we had with LeAnn's father as he slipped away into a mental fog. Words and meanings didn't always connect, but there still was an understanding of the main message, "We love you." We expressed that in words and deeds and sometimes by just sitting quietly beside him. Sometimes he responded with words we understood, and sometimes we saw it in his eyes.

It's the language of hospitality and caring, and it requires patience and bravery. You can only hear it and speak it if you stop what you are doing and make yourself present in the moment.

LeAnn was reading a book of quotes by Fred Rogers, and she read this one to me: "The purpose of life is to listen—to yourself, to your neighbor, to your world and to God—and when the time comes, to respond in as helpful a way as you can find . . . from within and without."[1]

Sometimes that response can be as simple and yet as powerful as standing on the sidewalk with a cup of coffee or sitting quietly on the edge of a bed.

Cleanup at 901

LeAnn and I took a few days off for a road trip, and when the mail finally caught up with us we were frustrated to find a code compliance letter in with all the usual junk mail. We were frustrated because we work really hard to keep our property in top shape.

Still, there was the letter highlighting two things that needed attention right away: house numbers on the back of our property and trimming trees and brush in the alley according to city standards of no more than a foot out from the property line and at least fourteen feet clearance above.

Keep in mind that our alley is of no real use because in our neighborhood all of our trash pickup is out front, and all our driveways and garages are out front, or in our case, on the side street. What's more, our alley isn't even paved. That means every week when I mow the yard, I mow the alley too—keeping clean a byway that no one uses.

Still, we complied and in fact the tree and brush trimming prompted us to go ahead and do some work in the backyard and alley that we had said we needed to do. We cleared out some thorny vines that were crawling up the trees and choking out the camellias and the leatherleaf mahonia. And we cleaned up tree limbs that were hanging almost head high over the backyard. For the city-required tree work in the alley, we flagged down a crew who was working at a neighbor's house. So now the alley was looking good and tidy, and we got some numbers to put on a sign to declare to no one in particular that, yes, this is 901.

All this cleanup at 901 took place in the midst of a national brush-clearing of sorts. In the wake of a horrific church massacre in Charleston, South Carolina, states and communities and neighborhoods mostly across the South had been looking at the brush and briars of history and considering what needs to be cleared out: Confederate flags, monuments to fallen Rebel soldiers, other reminders of a time in our nation's history when not all people had equal rights under the law.

As it happened, we got a big taste of this history while on that road trip before our yard cleanup. Weeks earlier, we had blocked out a few days and decided to visit Natchitoches, Louisiana—not knowing we would be touring old plantations in the aftermath of the Charleston shootings. But that's what we were doing, and we were pleased to have two excellent tour guides. One was a young black woman working through the Historically Black Colleges and Universities Initiative, a program of the National Parks Service; the other was a young white woman who has studied drama at Yale. Both were well versed and engaging as they shared the history of the plantations and the agrarian economy of the region in the nineteenth and early twentieth centuries.

From what I could tell, neither one editorialized or embellished. They both offered a straightforward telling of history. But as we walked and listened, I did wonder what thoughts and personal experiences they might be holding back behind the studied scripts they were following and the professionalism they were practicing. I can imagine that the black woman has endured her share of racism. And a white female Southerner at an Ivy League school in Connecticut might very well be subjected to slights and shames. I don't know.

Remove flags, take down monuments and statues, do all of that and more if you wish. That might change some attitudes and turn some hearts, or it might be akin to putting house numbers in an alley where no one walks. It seems to me the real brush that needs to be cleared out is ignorance, intolerance, poverty, greed, and prejudice of all types. These are the thorns that are hurting our nation and need our attention—including at 901.

Setting a Table

"How many of you can walk into your neighbor's house, take cookies out of their pantry, and then sit down at their table and eat them?"

That was a question Kristin Schell posed to participants at the annual Neighborhood Summit in our community on a Saturday morning. Schell is founder of the

Turquoise Table movement that promotes community and neighborliness through the placement of iconic turquoise picnic tables in front yards.

Schell asked her question, but no one raised their hand. And, of course, she already knew why: "Fifty percent of Americans don't know their neighbors. We don't know each other anymore," she said.

Anymore? That word hints that once upon a time we did know each other better than we do now. Schell grew up in Dallas and said she could still visualize the kitchen of her childhood home and those of her neighbors' houses. She could still hear the slamming of doors as friends and neighbors came and went.

"Life had a different pace. We knew those neighbors we could count on," she said.

Schell lives in Austin now, and a walk through her neighborhood after she'd been there a while brought the realization that she didn't know her neighbors. "I was part of that 50 percent," she said.

But then something interesting happened. She hosted a backyard barbecue for friends and didn't have room inside, so she ordered a couple of cheap picnic tables from Lowe's. When the delivery driver left a table in her front yard, she had a thought: "What if I left a table there?" And then she wondered, "What would it look like to plant the seeds of presence in our neighborhood?"

So, she painted the table turquoise, her favorite color, and within minutes a neighbor she'd never seen before stopped by and said she loved turquoise too.

"I couldn't have lived closer and I had never seen her before," said Schell.

Friends and strangers took notice of the table, and word spread. The tables began to multiply, and now there are thousands of turquoise tables in fifty states and thirteen countries.

We have a turquoise table on our corner lot, thanks to a ministry of engagement and hospitality at our church. But meeting the person who started the movement adds a layer of interest because she's not just one of those people from Austin who is living the mantra, "Keep Austin Weird." As it turns out, she wasn't intending to start a movement; she was just trying to bring back some of what makes being a neighbor not only enjoyable but also vital.

It sounds like there was a good measure of nostalgia in her desire, but she hints at a higher purpose.

"I know from Scripture that we are called to know our neighbors," she said. "We were created to live in community."

I know that instinctively, but it can still set me on edge. While LeAnn has the gift of hospitality and she shares it generously, I have the impediment of introversion and I can cling to it if allowed. So, LeAnn will "set the table" for guests and I'll follow her lead. But as it turns out, the turquoise table sort of runs itself. Maybe it's because of the bright color, or because of the fact that it's in the yard near the street, but people seem to notice it and come to it without much prompting. We've hosted some intentional events out there, but some of what we've done has been very low key and ad lib—and that brings people too.

Most surprising is that we've had a neighbor tell us they've seen people sitting at our table when we've done nothing at all. Just sitting, or perhaps resting? From what, we don't know: maybe a long walk, maybe a bad day?

That's an interesting development, but we'll need to be more watchful. Not in the "get off my yard!" kind of way, but in the "what can we do for you?" kind of way. Because being a good neighbor and being community requires some real interaction.

As Schell says: "We live in the digital age, and yet we have never been more lonely. I felt that loneliness. . . . There will never be an 'i-device' that can take the place of eye contact."

Red, White, and Blue

Every July 4th holiday we hang bunting on the front porch railing. The holiday always begins with a question: "Now . . . where did we put the bunting when we took it down last year?" And once we answer that question—in a box in the attic—then comes the second question: "How do we rig this?" We've had to invent a way to hang it so that it doesn't flop backward over the railing or bunch up and look like we're just drying our laundry.

Sadly, how to hang bunting on the railing is not the only thing that seems to have been forgotten in recent years. We've also forgotten things such as civility, compassion, respect, tolerance, empathy, patience, and many other qualities that have always been ways we define our nation and that contribute to our understanding of what we call community, civil society, and being good neighbors.

One year before Independence Day we were in Washington, D.C., and saw many shining examples of these qualities that have been hallmarks of the "American Way" and the "American Dream." I'm not talking about the endless acres of museums and monuments that a person could spend years trying to see. I'm talking about the everyday people we met who live and work in the midst of that boiling cauldron of democratic chaos and yet manage to keep their cool and their sense of community, for example:

• The Uber driver from Nepal who came to the United States to study business and is working in administration at a university, driving on weekends, and developing a business plan for a nonprofit agency to help people from his country come to America, gain an education, and return to Nepal to provide hope and opportunity there.

- The maître d' at a Greek restaurant who shared a little slice of his personal story and said, "Every day I am proud and honored to serve the people of the United States of America with respect and dignity." And yes, he did.
- The made-in-America owner/operator of a nighttime monuments tour who gave his heart and soul to his customers as he told our collective story of nationhood—warts and all—with enthusiasm and good humor.
- The docent at the Library of Congress, originally from Denmark, who shared her passion for literature, history, and architecture with a big smile and a twinkle in her eye.
- The young congressional interns who gamely led yet another group from Texas on a march through the crowded rotunda and halls of the Capitol.
- The airman at the Air Force Memorial who saw me crouching on the pavement, trying to frame a photo, and led me back thirty yards to show me the perfect spot to get the perfect picture.
- The security guard at the National Portrait Gallery who pointed out some details on a painting that we completely overlooked, and thereby transformed the viewing.
- The busy children's librarian at the Library of Congress who kept her promise and emailed LeAnn within days with information about a book she was looking for.
- The gracious member of Vienna Baptist Church who greeted us the way we should always remember to greet our guests.
- And the tens of thousands of fellow tourists who performed what I call "the museum shuffle" that is required in crowded quarters to keep from stepping on each other, and who said, "Excuse me" and "I'm sorry" at the slightest bump of elbows.

Those memories are the souvenirs I brought home from Washington that I don't want to put away in the attic and forget. Those are the American qualities—the God-given human qualities, actually—that I want to remember and do a better job of living and promoting.

Trick or Treat

A few days before Halloween, LeAnn and I went from door to door of every house in our neighborhood. We didn't ring doorbells, and we didn't come home with bags of candy. But it was "trick or treat" just the same because, well, neighborhoods can be scary and fun all at the same time.

It was a Monday afternoon and we were distributing flyers inviting folks to a community meeting on Saturday morning. There'd been quite a dustup over the future of the park that borders our neighborhood, and city staff wanted to restore some calm and civility to the process. They contacted me because I was the president of the voluntary neighborhood association.

Our neighborhood, called Embree, is a remnant of the town of Embree founded in 1886 and then merged with Duck Creek in 1891 to form the new town of Garland. We have houses built in the 1800s and pretty much every decade since then. Embree looks like a small town rather than a modern suburb. In some of the chatter on social media about the park, Embree was described as a bunch of "low-income retirees," but that is not true. We do have retirees, and we do have people of lower income. But we also have young people and middle agers, university administrators and landscapers, Ph.D. scholars and mechanics, writers and truck drivers, dental hygienists and woodcarvers, artists and accountants. We are black, white, and brown. We have people living in the house they grew up in, and newcomers like ourselves.

So, through this diverse neighborhood we walked, taping flyers to doors and mailboxes, being as quiet and unobtrusive as possible but also not avoiding encounters as they came, such as the man who shared the latest developments in his garden, or the young woman who gave an update on her fight with cancer. A couple working in their garage whom I'd never seen before looked at the flyer skeptically and asked, "Are you out politicking?" The answer was, "No." Another man came out into the yard to meet us and thank us for the invitation. A neighbor we know stopped in his truck and jokingly asked LeAnn if she was out "walking the streets," and another wished out loud that the city would just leave us alone.

Most of the houses were quiet at four in the afternoon, but that didn't stop me from tiptoeing across wooden porches so as not to draw any attention—especially at a few houses of an age and condition where it looked like there might be a Boo Radley inside the screen door. But just like in *To Kill a Mockingbird*, we've discovered that some of the Boos in our neighborhood are the ones you want beside you when things get tough.

We've made the same trek to get the word out for other meetings, and this time I gamely returned to a door with a sign peppered with blistering expletives telling the world they don't want to be bothered by anyone for any reason. Except for this note at the bottom: "Girl Scout cookies? Yes." The only house we avoided was one where, on previous occasions, the man emailed me or chased me down and said it was illegal to post notices in or near his mailbox.

Interestingly, many of the houses that I was hesitant to approach were decorated and ready for Halloween, which lets me know that my fear and hesitance are misplaced. I think the trick to getting along in a neighborhood such as ours is to treat everyone with the same respect, dignity, and trust that you would like in return. It's true in Embree, and I bet it's true in your neighborhood, too.

Impractical Hospitality

Two people live at our house. One is generous and hospitable. The other is hesitant and standoffish. You might doubt that, but it shows up in the smallest, most innocuous ways.

One late afternoon when the brush and bulky trash truck finally came up our street, I ran downstairs to watch it from the front window. The truck comes every week, and I had a small pile of brush and branches that I had put off dragging to the curb for weeks, and now I wanted to make sure it got picked up.

"It's the pitchfork truck," I shouted to LeAnn as I looked out the front windows. I said that because on this regularly scheduled day, a big truck with a big claw came down the street and stopped in front of our neighbor's house. The driver got out, climbed up on top, sat in the control chair, and maneuvered the claw down to pick up their pile of brush and load it in the back. Then he climbed down and drove away, leaving our smaller pile untouched. The pitchfork truck, on the other hand, is an old-style garbage truck with a man who jumps off the back and uses a genuine pitchfork to stab a pile of brush and lift it into the back of the truck.

As I watched the man maneuver the pile to get the largest amount possible—like a hungry man working a plate of spaghetti with a fork—LeAnn came out from her office and said, "I'll give them some cookies." She had baked some toffee cookies especially for me a few days earlier, and we had some to spare.

"Oh . . . don't do that," I said. Somewhere in my too-practical mind I reasoned that these two men were running late and were too busy to enjoy the niceties of cookies rushed out from the front door of a random house. But then something clicked inside me: I realized I was stifling LeAnn's natural gift of hospitality. While I would never think to give a city worker a handful of cookies, especially not while I was standing in judgment of how well he completed his job, it was for LeAnn exactly who she is and what she does for anyone and everyone all the time.

"Don't listen to me," I said, ashamed of myself. "Do what you want to do."

And she did, and not because I gave her any sort of permission; we don't roll that way, and I wouldn't have it any other way. LeAnn ran out with a bag of cookies and handed it up to the man as the truck started to pull away. And then the driver honked his horn and the man jumped off the back, ran to the front, and climbed into the cab, and the truck drove away down the street.

I went out later and picked up the twigs and dry leaves left behind on the lawn. "They never get it all," I thought, but then the thought evaporated as I imagined two men enjoying the simple pleasure of homemade cookies on a hot afternoon.

The Civil Center

I find myself in a challenging time. Late in my professional career I've been given opportunities to share some thoughts and meditations, and it's been a blessing to me in many ways. It has stretched me as a writer and challenged me as an introvert. It has prompted me to examine my faith—to take it apart like a mechanic who dismantles an engine and inspects the parts. Much of my writing has been "reports" on what I am learning.

The challenge, however, is that during the time I have been doing this, social media has sprung up as a powerful force in our world. I don't know if historians looking back will equate it with Gutenberg's printing press, but comparisons may be appropriate. While the printing press put more information into the hands of the masses, social media has made everyone a Gutenberg with the potential of reaching a global audience.

This means lots of people are talking, and they're talking about things I'm interested in and have opinions about. Through their posts I've discovered that some of my friends and followers and those I follow are in stark disagreement with me on many issues. There's nothing wrong with that; disagreement is natural and healthy and can lead to new ideas and solutions to problems. But social media doesn't always promote healthy dialogue; conversations too often devolve into angry shouting. The worst is Twitter because the character limit doesn't allow for context and shading. And the tweets and retweets string out forever, with total strangers engaged in verbal fistfights. Everyone is shouting, but no one is listening.

Some days it takes every ounce of restraint I can muster to not react to something I read that I believe is over-the-top, outrageous exaggeration or that I just disagree with strongly. I quite literally have to step away from the computer or turn off my device to resist the urge to say something I will regret almost immediately. I've been so tempted to shout back that I've unfollowed some people on Twitter and Facebook.

My problem is, this little light of mine—as the old song goes—can be as gaudy and ugly as anyone's. So I'm keeping the lamp shade on, not because I'm better than anyone but because I have an unwritten contract with myself and the people who read my words that I won't spread the negativity. I have an opportunity to share God's love, and I could destroy it in an instant with a few careless words.

There's a place in our public dialogue for well-informed people with well-crafted words to shine light on injustice, prejudice, and other ills. History is full of strong men and women, liberals and conservatives, all colors and shapes, who have helped us move forward by illuminating our failings and weaknesses. You know their names. Their big lights shine brightly for all the right reasons. Meanwhile, many of us need to practice restraint or at least stop and think before we speak instead of shouting at each other from the loud left or the raucous right.

Anyone care to join me in the civil center?

Backpacks, Boats, and Hands

A highlight of worship at our church every year on a Sunday in late August is the Blessing of the Backpacks, where school children are invited to bring their backpacks and book bags to the front of the church for a special litany and prayer. The kids may not realize it, but it's actually a blessing for them; the backpacks just represent the journey of learning and growing they are starting. They're joined at the chancel by teachers who guide them on this journey.

But what about the rest of us? What about those of us who carry briefcases and toolboxes, who work with pens and keyboards, who wear coveralls and aprons, who wield scalpels and hammers? What about the work we do that sometimes seems small and insignificant but nonetheless may have the power to change lives through the sharing of God's love and mercy? Is there a time of blessing for us too?

There's an age-old tradition in port cities called the Blessing of the Fleet, where ships and their crews are blessed before going out to sea for the annual catch. One such blessing goes like this:

> Most gracious Lord, who numbered among your apostles the fishermen Peter, Andrew, James and John, we pray you to consecrate this boat to righteous work in your name. Guide the captain at her helm. So prosper her voyages that an honest living may be made. Watch over her passengers and crew and bring them to a safe return. And the blessing of God Almighty, the Father, the Son and the Holy Spirit, be upon this vessel and all who come aboard, this day and forever. Amen.[2]

It's a beautiful prayer but not as fitting for workers in a landlocked city. And, it would be logistically impossible to have a blessing service for all the varied ways that we work and make a living today. But that doesn't mean it shouldn't be done or can't be done in some form or fashion—perhaps alone, with coworkers, or with friends in the same field.

There are many fine prayers of blessing over the work you do that can be found on the internet. Following is one written by Diann Neu, a liturgist and therapist working in Maryland. I like it because it focuses on the one thing that we all have in common: our hands. You might consider praying this or a similar prayer. Your work year may not start alongside the school year, but there's never a bad time to pause a moment and ask for God's blessings over the work you do, no matter what it may be.

Blessed be These Hands
Blessed be the works of your hands,
O Holy One.
Blessed be these hands that have touched life.
Blessed be these hands that have nurtured creativity.
Blessed be these hands that have held pain.
Blessed be these hands that have embraced with passion.
Blessed be these hands that have tended gardens.
Blessed be these hands that have closed in anger.
Blessed be these hands that have planted new seeds.
Blessed be these hands that have harvested ripe fields.
Blessed be these hands that have cleaned, washed, mopped, scrubbed.
Blessed be these hands that have become knotty with age.
Blessed be these hands that are wrinkled and scarred from doing justice.
Blessed be these hands that have reached out and been received.
Blessed be these hands that hold the promise of the future.
Blessed be the works of your hands,
O Holy One.[3]

Strength for the Journey

I was out mowing the lawn on the morning of July 4th and looked up to see Orlando, our Cuban refugee neighbor, giving me a thumbs-up from across the street. I call him a "refugee" without really knowing his story. I know his daughter came here some years ago, met and married a man from Mexico while they both worked at a large downtown hotel, and eventually brought her parents over. Refugees, immigrants, migrants, legal, illegal—I just don't know. They're our neighbors and good neighbors at that, and, like many of us home-grown types, they are mostly private and keep to themselves.

I returned the thumbs-up and kept working until a while later when I made a turn with the mower and there stood Orlando, holding up a tiny cup and saucer and grinning from ear to ear.

It's hard to describe what I feel at these moments—and I've had them before—but it's pretty much a storm of competing emotions:

• irritation—because my carefully scheduled mowing routine has been disrupted
• anxiety—because Orlando doesn't speak English and I don't speak Spanish
• fear—because I'm sweating buckets and I really don't think a shot of strong Cuban coffee is the best thing in these conditions

- admiration—because Orlando always makes the first brave move
- anticipation—because there is usually an unexpected discovery in these meetings

So I let go of the mower handle, which cut off the motor, and I walked the few feet to where Orlando was standing. We traded "good mornings" and he handed me the cup and saucer, but there was a handshake at the same time and we almost spilled it all. Then came nervous laughter and the beginning of me taking small sips while he stood and watched. And then slowly, we began an awkward, broken conversation about the weather and the work I was doing—at least I think that's what we were talking about. A little wind blew up and I said, "the breeze feels good," and he motioned with his hands and said "brisa," and for a moment we were in the same place.

Orlando's wife was watching us from the porch across the street, and she shouted something to him in Spanish. He pointed to my cup and then to our house and asked, "Señora?" I think he was asking if LeAnn would like some coffee too, so I said no and made a drinking motion and a swirl around my head and said, "crazy." My meaning was that LeAnn doesn't do well with caffeine, but Orlando may have received a different message from me.

When I emptied the cup, Orlando gave me a double thumbs-up and raised his shoulders, forearms, and fists. I interpreted that to mean the coffee would provide strength for the rest of my work, so I acted out running while pushing the mower. He nodded and laughed, and then his wife spoke again from across the street. Orlando raised up his shirt to reveal a large scar up under his arm and flesh that was red as a beet. He struggled a moment but found the word "radiation" and then formed a small ball with his hands, which looked to me like a tumor. "Cancer?" I asked, and he answered, "lymphoma."

My mind flashed back to a time maybe six months earlier when I saw what looked like the whole family surrounding the door of a car that had driven up and them helping someone out of the passenger seat and slowly up the walk and into the house. They have a lot of extended family and friends so I couldn't see who it was, but now I know it was Orlando.

Like I said earlier, I don't know if Orlando is a refugee, migrant, immigrant, citizen, or something else. But I do know that he is flesh and blood just like me and is susceptible to all that can threaten our humanity, whether it be illness, injustice, or indifference. I also know he is a fighter because that's what any of us is when our survival is at stake.

When the little coffee cup was empty and we had run out of words, I handed Orlando the cup and saucer. I offered him my best version of "gracias," and he worked up a stilted but earnest, "Happy Fourth of July."

Orlando turned toward his home, and I returned to my work. As I pushed the mower, I replayed the visit in my head, and then I had a thought and let the motor die again. Before going out, LeAnn had asked me to check the tomatoes, so I grabbed the blue garden bucket and picked a dozen or so Romas and cherries. Then she and I carried the bucket across the street where it seemed like the entire family met us at the door.

I believe tomatoes can make you strong, too.

Be Still and Listen

There we were, faces red, nose to nose:

"They haven't tested the soil and I know it's contaminated," he said.

"Yes, they have. He showed us the five-hundred-page report," I answered.

"And I'm going to read it."

"Then read it and see for yourself and quit saying they haven't done it."

If I wasn't shouting those last words, I was at least talking in a sharp staccato that anyone nearby could have heard. But few people were listening because most were leaving the meeting. They'd had enough.

The community I'd lived in for just a few years and was learning to love was fighting over a park. Really? Yes, the big, beautiful park in the center of town and bordering our neighborhood was facing changes, and people were fighting over what those changes should be. They also were fighting over who and how and when those types of decisions should be made. It's ironic: A park is supposed to be a place of rest and recreation, but our park had become a battleground of accusations and insults.

It's a microcosm of our society today. From border to border and from coast to coast, we just seem lost right now. We've lost our sense of civility. Pick a topic—any topic—and we're laying blame and calling names without consequence because the truth is not important. What's important is being loud and being first and promoting our interpretation of what's right. It's fueled by social media that's unsociable and traditional media that's become sloppy.

We're lost, and we need to find our way back to a place of trust and peace. Talking won't get us there as long as we desire to have the first word or the last word or to be the loudest. We need to step down and be the one who listens. More than that, we just need to be still.

It's often said that when you are desperately lost you should stay where you are so the searchers can find you. If you keep moving around, you can't be found. But if you stay still, the searchers will eliminate places to look and eventually find you. And if you are quiet, you can help; you can hear the searchers drawing near, call out to them, and be found.

My prayer for my community and for yours is that we will remember how to be still and to listen.

Random, Awkward Acts of Kindness

It was LeAnn's idea and a good one: sit at our turquoise table and offer cold bottled water and bags of chips and crackers to the high school kids who stream down our street when school lets out. We wouldn't put up a sign; we'd just be out there and try to get their attention, which is no small feat with kids who are awkward and hesitant and are prone to tune out the world with headphones.

"So, what will we say?" LeAnn asked, which I found unusual because she has the gift of hospitality like no one I've ever known.

"I don't know," I answered—and I truly didn't know. Hospitality is not my gift; hesitance and hiding are more my speed. But I do have the gift of trusting and going along with one of LeAnn's plans.

And so we waited, with LeAnn sitting at the table the way it was meant to be sat, and me sitting on the top of the table with my feet on the seat in what I called "the cool dude position," although I wasn't feeling cool at all. But then the first lone kid came along and that set the pattern for our encounters. LeAnn said, "Hi, would you like some snacks and water for your walk home?" And I dipped into the ice chest and held up a bottle of water as if to say, "Yes, we really do have bottled water and this is what it looks like."

The results were mixed. The first lone kid did exactly what I might have done: she jaywalked away from us and shook her head "no." Others soon followed. A few walked up boldly, but most had to be coaxed a little. Out of a group of four, two came and two waited at the corner. A kid with a lollipop stick in his mouth took some hard candy. Some thanked us, and some said the same with a silent nod of the head.

When the kids quit coming, we counted and found we'd handed out just nine bottles of water and fewer bags of chips. As we carried our goods back inside, LeAnn said that someday years from now one of those kids may remember a hot day in the first week of school when a strange couple sitting at a turquoise table was handing out snacks.

"Yes, we were modeling awkward hospitality," I said. And I was learning a few things in the process:

• LeAnn's voice can penetrate headphones.
• Kids today are as hesitant and shy as I was at that age.
• Apparently, it's cool to wear a hoodie when it's 98 degrees outside.

• Awkward goes both ways and knows no age.

• I'm no more comfortable making the first move than when I was sixteen.

The high school effort was in some ways a practice for our community's Labor Day parade, which began at the park a couple of blocks from our house. LeAnn marched in the parade with her high school band and remembers how exhausting it was, so we set up in time to catch parade participants as they walked back to their cars.

We had more takers this time: band members who were hungry and thirsty, drill teamers who were parched and wanted to pose for pictures, an ROTC cadet who took some water while chatting on the phone, families who had come to watch the parade and appreciated an energy boost until lunchtime. We tried but failed to stop a trailer load of candy-colored clowns, but we did coax a visit from a band member wearing a sousaphone almost as big as himself. He started to bend over to get a water bottle but asked for help when he realized his center of gravity was too high.

None of these people—the high schoolers and parade watchers—were our neighbors in the literal sense, as in living next door or down the street. They were all walking toward their own neighborhoods or to their cars to return to their neighborhoods and their families. But they were neighbors in the broader sense that they inhabit our community and our world.

We'll try the after-school handouts again sometime, and maybe we'll feel less awkward and more comfortable and confident, or maybe we won't. But that's okay because there's plenty of room in community for awkward. In a way that's sort of what makes a community interesting.

Joining the Club

During our annual joint birthday week, LeAnn and I visited a chain restaurant we rarely go to, but they're known for steaks and that seemed like a good way to celebrate. When the server came to our table, we realized he had served us once before because he has the same name as our youngest nephew. But we also realized it had been almost two years since our last visit because on that night the restaurant was having a benefit for that server and his family. His parents had died and two of his six siblings were seriously injured while driving home from a camping trip. He had not been on the trip, and at age twenty-three he had become the head of the family.

On that benefit night, he didn't serve us but we watched with admiration as he served his tables and accepted the well wishes of friends and strangers. We could see in his eyes that he was overwhelmed by the attention, not to mention the weight of the tragedy that still was fresh.

On this return visit, we didn't say anything about it until our meal was finished and he asked if we wanted to join the restaurant's frequent diner club. We don't usually do that, but this time we said yes, and we admitted that we hadn't been there in two years, and in fact the last time we were there was during the benefit for him. And then came the awkward question: "So, how've you been? Has life been relatively okay, considering?"

Slowly but without hesitation, he said it had been tough, and then he shared some of the past two years, including that his six younger siblings were all okay and were being raised by their grandparents now. He said he sees them when he can but he's working on a career at the restaurant chain and will probably transfer to another location as an assistant manager.

When we got home, I did a little sleuthing on the internet and found a news story that gave the how and when of the tragedy that took the server's parents and put two siblings in the hospital with life-threatening injuries. And then I found him on Facebook and read his postings of the slow but steady recovery of his two siblings. I also saw how before the accident, there was the typical carefree and sometimes inappropriate postings of a young man with a bright, sunny life ahead. And after the accident and recovery, there was a slow return to those carefree postings. But that might have just been a masking of real life because all his postings ended abruptly months earlier, perhaps reflecting the sharpened focus of a young man who is getting serious about the future.

LeAnn and I shared with each other later that we both were wanting to speak to him at the table but didn't want to pry until the club invite provided an opening. I'm mostly an introvert, but I have these weird moments when I feel compelled to ask the awkward question. Perhaps in this case it was a remembrance of my own loss and how I didn't want to talk about it but sometimes I was hungry for someone to ask.

As it happened, at the end of our conversation, our server said, "People rarely say anything to me about it, but thanks for asking."

I do believe there's some healing that happens when we talk about these things. Sometimes it may take someone stepping out on faith, joining the club, and asking the awkward question. And who knows? Now that we've joined the club, we might go to that restaurant more often. And if he's changed locations, we might even go to the one where that brave young man is the manager. It might be good to see how he's doing.

THE HUMAN FAMILY:
ACROSS TOWN AND AROUND THE GLOBE

"To err is human; to forgive, divine." I've erred a lot, so I know where that puts me. As humans we make mistakes for sure, but the biggest mistake we make is when we forget or discount each other's humanity. Like it or not, we're all in this together.

The human family has claimed every person who has ever lived. Every member has the same basic genetic makeup, but our experiences are wildly different. And there lies the rub: how to relate to those who come out of different experiences.

Pursuit of Happiness

A period of extended travel had me considering the interesting patterns you find when you try to connect the dots.

First stop on this trip was Cimarron, New Mexico, for my nephew's high school graduation. He finished first in his class, gave a great speech, and we were all so proud of him. Because the class was small—just thirty-one kids—we got to know more about each of them. Everyone in his class had a plan for the future: twenty-six were going to college, two were going to trade school, two were entering the workforce, and one was joining the army. All had their sights set on doing something meaningful with their lives.

I arrived home from that trip at noon on a Monday, shook out my duffle bag and reloaded because the next morning I was on a plane to the Dominican Republic. Nine of us from our church went to see firsthand what two great organizations—Esperanza International and Buckner International—were doing to help transform lives with microfinancing of small businesses and developing schools and community centers. I came home moved by the spirit of the people there who were working extremely hard and stretching the few resources they had to build better lives for their families and communities.

And then a few days later I gathered with friends at Flag Pole Hill in Dallas to picnic and hear the Dallas Symphony's annual Memorial Day concert with patriotic tunes and fireworks. It was a night to be thankful for our freedom and prosperity made possible in large part by the sacrifices of others.

We Americans sometimes think we invented the idea of "life, liberty, and the pursuit of happiness." After all, it's handwritten in ink in our Declaration of Independence. But if you read the entire sentence before that phrase, you'll recall that it says: "We hold these truths to be self-evident, that *all* men are created equal, that they are *endowed by their creator* with certain unalienable Rights, that among these are Life, Liberty, and the pursuit of Happiness" (emphasis added).

In other words, this is not exclusively an American ideal; it's a universal desire, placed in every human who has ever breathed by our common creator—whether in the hills of Cimarron, the farms of Vasquez, or the streets of Dallas. That being the case, it seems to me that when we see other people struggling to achieve their dreams, we should either pitch in and help in a dignified way or at least clear a path and get out of the way so they can succeed on their own. Above all else, we should work to remove the impediments to our neighbors' desire for prosperity and happiness, and certainly we should never be an impediment ourselves. Not everyone will succeed in the same way, but everyone has the inalienable right to try.

Shared Loss

We all will experience loss at some point—parent, spouse, child, friend, sibling, grandparent, pet, job, health. And while from the outside it may look like some losses are more significant than others, the measuring sticks are meaningless when you're on the inside. When it's your loss, it hurts badly, and that's all you know.

I was on a DART train one Saturday, sitting behind a man who clearly was stricken. His head was hanging, his shoulders were shaking, and when he turned for a moment to see if anyone was watching him, I could see the tears streaming down his face. When he saw that I'd seen him, he cleared his throat and asked me, "Have you ever lost someone?" I answered, "Yes." He turned away for a moment and then turned back and said, "My neighbors think I'm crazy, but my cat died, and I just don't know what to do now. She was all I had."

"I don't think you're crazy at all," I said. "She was your companion, your family, and now you're lonely and you miss her." He nodded, and then he asked, "Who did you lose?" I answered, "My wife."

He immediately began to backpedal: "I'm so sorry, you must think I'm a fool to be crying over a cat when you've lost so much more." I said, "Oh no, your loss is as big as mine because it's *your* loss, and nobody can judge what that means to you."

I believed that then, and I believe it even more today. I've lost a spouse, a sister, grandparents, a high school buddy, favorite pets, and beloved mentors. Each loss has been uniquely significant and life-changing. I don't place one above the other because at the time, each one hurt terribly.

The good news is that each loss has also been a learning experience and an opportunity to grow. Each loss brings us closer to our own humanity and our brotherhood and sisterhood with those around us. The more we lose, the more we understand pain, and the more we're willing to give to others when their time of pain comes.

Each loss leaves a hole in the heart that seemingly can never be filled, but if we're paying attention and we're open, we find that God, family, and friends are eager to fill that hole with something wonderful: their love.

Finding the Pitch

It began with a single, soft note . . . a brief pause . . . and then a perfectly formed chord of four, six, or even eight notes. And from that single chord a perfectly lovely melody was built, ebbing and flowing, rising and falling, drifting through the symphony hall and into the ears and down into the souls of all who were listening. It was moving and stirring. And it all began with a single, soft note.

Most of the selections by the magnificent choir from St. Olaf College were sung a cappella, and I found myself watching each time for a young man on the second row to render that single, soft note from a pitch pipe before each piece. At first I thought two things: either he's the most trusted member of the choir, or he's a freshman and this is some kind of initiation ritual. Later it was revealed by the choir's director that the young man is a gifted composer and arranger—the choir sang one of his compositions—so it's likely that playing the pitch pipe is a role of high honor and trust.

It's a simple task, really, but a critical one. Without that first perfect note, the choristers might start in different places and fill the hall with dissonance. Even if they have perfect pitch—and many surely do—some might start a half step high or low of the intended mark. They might eventually find their way to harmony, but there'd be a moment of bent notes, swooping, and searching before they all got in tune. Or they might have wandered aimlessly until the director silenced them to start again. And if not trustworthy or serious, the young man with the pitch pipe might have blown the wrong note and started them off equally lost.

To get it right, the person with the pitch pipe must play the right note, and the choristers fanned out around him must listen intently, draw that sound into their mind, place their own first note alongside what they've just heard, and then voice it as precisely as they imagined it. It's actually a complex process.

I'm not a singer and you may not be either, but we all listen to others at different times and in different ways in search of the perfect pitch for our lives. We key off others as we seek harmony in our relationships, careers, vocations, and daily movement through this world.

None of us are solo performers; we interact with others all the time. So . . . who are we listening to, and how well are we listening? Are we being led to harmony, or to dissonance? And, who is listening to us?

A Day on the Journey

I failed to read the fine print and didn't realize until I got to the airport at five thirty in the morning that my one-stop flight to Washington actually included brief stops in Little Rock and Kansas City in addition to Chicago. The people paying my way made the arrangements, so I couldn't really complain. Besides, there was much to observe and learn along the way.

Dallas to Little Rock

Sitting in front of me were two young businessmen who spoke with authority and used terms such as "negative arbitrage" and "game on." Interestingly, the latter was used by one to describe his battle with his thirteen-year-old who wanted a smartphone. With gelled hair and starched shirt, he clearly had the world by the tail.

As the sun rose, a storm lit up the tops of clouds on the horizon, and a shooting star briefly blazed. In my earphones, David Gilmour sang, "Where We Start," about a long, languid journey into the woods.

On the ground in Little Rock, the man next to me called his office and asked his co-workers to "process the pay vouchers." He reported on the trade show he attended and went through a stack of business cards he had collected. "Yes, I got the motorcycle license, but I'm not feeling very confident yet." He was wearing one of those brightly stenciled long-sleeve T-shirts that motocross racers wear. He was also wearing jeans and penny loafers, identifying him as the dependable boss back at the office but a rebel out on the road.

Little Rock to Chicago

Two women behind me never had met before, but they woke up that morning one street apart in a Dallas suburb. "What a small world. We could have commuted together," one said. She had been visiting her brother, and the other was a newcomer to town, having transferred after her husband died. "I love Dallas," she said. "The women are so jazzy with all their jewelry and big hair."

Above the clouds it was sunny, but the pilot warned of cold rain and turbulence on the way into Chicago. Despite the warning, the ride was smooth, but we spent thirty minutes in the thick gray clouds before landing in the rain.

In Chicago, I walked a mile to change planes. I picked up coffee and a giant oatmeal cookie for breakfast and juiced up my phone so I could text LeAnn and answer emails. Everyone around me was doing the same or sleeping. An announcement on the public address system provided important instructions on the proper way to sneeze.

Chicago to Washington, D.C.

Boarding the plane, I learned that we weren't stopping in Kansas City after all. Good news, but the flight was packed. Maybe it was the gloomy weather, or the cramped quarters, or the fact that we were no longer in friendly Texas, but no one was chatting amiably anymore. The serious mood put me on guard. They told us to turn off our cell phones, and I ratted out a woman two rows up because I could see a green light blinking in the top of her purse.

I wanted to arrive safely. About fifteen minutes after takeoff, we burst through the clouds into the sunlight and I could hear people talking again. Interesting how the sun can do that. Landing in D.C., I was eager to get to work so I could turn around and go home.

What's the point of this uneventful travelogue? We're all on a journey. Some of it we control, and much of it we don't. We'll meet fellow travelers and maybe bond for a while or perhaps a lifetime. There'll be bright sunrises and dark clouds, smooth rides and turbulence, real battles and invented conflicts, shooting stars and planeloads of travelers headed in other directions. Some stops will be scheduled, and some will be unexpected. Through it all, we can't really complain because the one who gave us life made the arrangements. It's good to be along for the ride.

The Value of Being Nice

I left the dentist with tears in my eyes. No, it wasn't because of pain, and it wasn't because of the bill. But the visit did touch a tender nerve.

You see, my longtime dentist told me he was retiring so he could spend more time with grandkids and traveling. He was bringing in a young man to take over his practice, and he assured me I was going to like the new "big dog" because he was sharp and smart. My response: "If you handpicked him, then I know he's a kind man too."

That's when I lost it. My point, which I made when I regained my composure, was that a few years earlier when my wife Debra died, the dentist was very kind to me during my first visit as a widower. I don't recall exactly what he did or said, but I still remember the feeling I had when I left his office that day—that things were going to be okay. On a subsequent visit, when I asked him about a potential tooth problem, he said, "My advice to you is to go out and have a great day." That's the kind of man he was, so with this visit being my last time to see him, I wanted him to know how much I appreciated that. His always-upbeat reply was, "And you remarried, and life is good." And yes, it is.

From there I rode the train downtown to Inge's Barber Shop for a haircut. I'd been visiting Inge and Lydia (who cuts my hair) for ten years, and like my dentist they've lifted me up in ways I can't define. Maybe it's just that they are so dependably and consistently nice, but I've always left their shop feeling like my attitude has been straightened up along with my sideburns.

All I can do to repay any of these folks is to be loyal and continue going to the old neighborhood for a cleaning and downtown for a trim. And perhaps I can learn from them and make sure I'm being kind to the people I meet every day, no matter whether they're friends or relations, strangers or clients. Because sometimes a haircut is more than just a haircut, and a trip to the dentist is more than just a checkup.

And the Winner Is . . .

Each year between Christmas and Easter there is another season that consumes many people: Hollywood award season, when people who make a lot of money to put on costumes and pretend they are someone else enjoy a giant group hug and celebrate each other for being such wonderful make-believe play actors. They dress up in designer gowns and tuxes and then gush and blush and place each other on pedestals and proclaim that theirs is the most noble of all professions, which of course is the reason they merit all the attention and kudos. And in the process, some of them are rude and profane, while others are serious and earnest as they tell us how we should be more kind and generous and genuine—like the characters they portray.

While the celebrities party the night away at their victory balls, the rest of us turn off our televisions and crawl into bed because we have to get up early and go to our real jobs with real people to face real issues and real drama. And some of these real people do the kind of real work that the Hollywood play actors pretend to do, but it is much different because the real people don't go home to a hotel at night to read the next day's script, and they don't recover from the hard work of pretending by taking a hiatus at Lake Como in Italy. In fact, they may not take a break for years because on top of their real work they raise families and help their neighbors and volunteer at the school and church. And they most definitely don't dress up and go to award shows because their real jobs don't have award shows.

My point is that during this season of fawning over the make-believers who entertain us—and yes, there is a value to their entertainment—why not take a moment to offer a word of gratitude and thanks to the real people around us who are truly worthy of our appreciation and respect.

For each of us that is a different cast of characters. For me it is my spouse, my parents, and close family and friends, of course, but it also is: my neighbors who support and help each other, the people who serve me at my favorite restaurants, the woman who cuts my hair, the man at the small shop who sells me office supplies, the folks at the nursery who help us keep the flowers and vegetables growing, the people who built our house and still check on us, and all the people who work behind the scenes at church to ensure we have a wonderful place for worship and fellowship.

For all of these and more, I have no gold statuettes to offer. But I hope you'll accept this heartfelt, enthusiastic "Thank You!"

Playing It Forward

In a sermon our pastor talked about a golfer whose coach was trying to teach him to hit down on the ball. If you want the ball to go up, you have to hit down. The golfer was a "picker"—one who wants to pick the ball up with the club so as not to disturb the turf beneath it. In frustration the coach finally said, "Leave some evidence behind that you have been here, man." Meaning: don't be afraid to leave a divot. In the context of the sermon, our pastor was saying: we, as a church, should dig deep with our mission endeavors and leave positive signs of our presence in the community.

When I first tried my hand at golf, I tried to play cleanly too. I ended up "topping" the ball—hitting the top of it, which caused it to roll forward an embarrassingly short distance or squirt out in some wild direction, including behind me. While I've never become proficient at golf, I at least have learned that if I focus on hitting down on the ball and not worrying about tearing up the grass, I have a better chance of getting airborne and then I can start to work on distance and direction.

Now, if I can add a stroke to our pastor's illustration, I'll say that most golf courses don't want you to tear up the earth and move on. The ones that care about their fairways send every golf cart out with a pail of sand and a little scoop. Yes, you should swing under the ball and take out a nice healthy divot, but then you should take a moment and fill the divot with sand. That way, when the grass grows back in, it will be level with the surrounding turf and not become a permanent pockmark that will catch other balls or get washed out by the next hard rain and become bigger. So, sometimes the benefit of "leave some evidence behind that you have been here" depends on what you leave behind.

When I was in Scouts, we camped almost monthly and were governed by the philosophy of "leave the campsite better than you found it." That didn't mean just cleaning up our trash or "filling our divots" as it were; that meant leaving a pile of wood next to the fire pit, clearing some brush from the trail, leaving arrows made of stones that point to water or other resources. The idea was to provide a better experience for the next troop that visited. You see pro golfers on TV doing the same: they'll walk up to the green and fix a ball mark even when it has no bearing on their next stroke. It's just good etiquette.

So, what signs of our presence do we leave behind on our daily journey? Do we leave raw divots that will wash out and get bigger with the next storm? Do we leave depleted resources? Do we leave the wrappings and trappings of our affluence? Or do we leave our home, our neighborhood, our church, our community, our world better than we found it?

To Whom Much Has Been Entrusted . . .

So this is the scenario: You're out for a Saturday evening walk and are approached by a man and woman who tell you they are homeless. He says he can make it on the street, but he says the woman, who he just met, is not so able. She is from out of state and has no ID because her purse was stolen. Without an ID, she can't stay at one of the big downtown Dallas shelters. She looks exhausted, can barely speak, and uses her hands to hold on clothing that is too big and probably not hers.

As you're hearing their story, you're standing on a street corner within two blocks of all the big-name denominational churches in town. All are closed, except the one that meets on Saturday night. You walk the couple over there and find that the last members remaining are turning off the lights and leaving. You ask if the pastor is there; he is, and you tell him the situation. He says that the church has nothing to offer at that time of night, and then he tells you privately that he has dealt with the man before and hints that he is uncertain of his honesty.

The pastor suggests that you check with the fire department, so you leave the couple sitting on the curb at the church and walk a couple of blocks to a fire station, where a fire crew is just returning from a call. You tell them the story and they say they have nothing to offer but suggest calling the 2-1-1 community services hotline.

You call 2-1-1 and you learn that no services are open or available at that hour. You also get confirmation that the big downtown shelters will not take people who have no ID. You go back to the couple and tell them that you've come up empty. You offer them the twelve dollars you have in your pocket, and the man declines it and begins a rant about how so-called "caring churches" and "people of God" don't really care and aren't modeling God's love at all. He says that in thirty-one days when he gets his six-figure military pension, he's going to open a ministry and mission that truly cares.

You become irritated and practically shout at him, "That's fine, but right now this is all we have for you; all we can give you is paper." You shove the money into his hand. "Please take it. It won't get you a room, but at least it will get you something to eat. Please."

You are frustrated and irritated because there is nothing you can do. You also are torn because you, in fact, have two beds within walking distance—but . . . it just doesn't feel safe. The man is a big talker, and the pastor you met raised your skepticism. And the woman? Well, as she walked with you she whispered through her fatigue that she had been in and out of jail but didn't say why. On top of that, you have bad memories of that time twenty-five years earlier when you tried to help someone on the street, got too close, and found yourself on a twelve-month tumble into manipulation and lies. You won't let that happen again.

Finally, this man agrees that there is nothing more to be done and takes the money you have offered. He asks you to pray with them, and while he asks for God's mercy for better days and forgiveness for unnamed sins, you want to interrupt him and tell him, "This isn't because of your sins; it's because we have failed as a community." But you keep that to yourself and let him confess his faith, which feels truer than your own in that moment.

You shake hands. He thanks you for your time, and she thanks you for trying to help. You walk away and don't look back. You're relieved that it is over but shaken that there was no real solution.

This happened to LeAnn and me on a Saturday night on the streets of downtown Garland. We were irritated by the interruption of our evening walk, frustrated by the total lack of services in the heart of a city of more than 240,000 people, and embarrassed by a seeming lack of faith and courage on our part. We were convicted, sickened, frightened, saddened, and shamed all at once.

There is no moral to this story, no quick solutions, no bold recommendations—just a weary acknowledgment that we have a huge dilemma in our communities. It is private and public, spiritual and physical, financial and logistical. It can't be resolved easily, but it demands better solutions than twelve dollars and a street-corner prayer on a hot Saturday night.

Chaos and Comfort

On a Thursday evening, storms blew through North Texas, peeling back roofs and splitting trees. Our home and those in most of our neighborhood were spared serious damage, but LeAnn's parents were without power. We navigated dark streets and piles of debris to bring them back to the light and comfort of our house for the night.

Friday morning was so different. The air was crisp and there was not a cloud in the sky. As I worked at my desk, I heard a mixture of sounds that caused me to run downstairs and out onto the porch. Somewhere down the street a whining chainsaw was turning broken trees into orderly piles. And from the north, the carillon at the Methodist church was playing its morning medley of hymns.

Chainsaws and chimes, chaos and comfort—fraternal twins that accompany many of our days. Usually they visit us separately, but sometimes they come at the same time. When they do, the results are intermingling joy and sorrow, peace and fear. It takes a steady faith to lean toward the hope of joy and peace. Sometimes it takes a family or a community pulling together.

The next Sunday morning at church we sang, prayed, and shared Communion as we normally do, but the presence of news media covering the story of Ebola in our community was a strong reminder that faith and hope share the pew with fear and anxiety. Cameras or no cameras, on any given Sunday any number of us may be suffering behind our reverent demeanor.

As if that Sunday morning was not full enough, that afternoon we stood at the bedside of a beloved cousin who suffered and fought disease far too long. The room became hushed when we thought he was taking his last breaths, but it wasn't time yet and the holy silence and tears gave way to stories and laughter about a life lived well. He did finally depart in the wee hours, but not before his mother said, "You won: You got there first."

For her, God's promise of eternal peace is the ultimate comfort amid the chaos of this life. Let it be so for us as well.

Darkness to Light

A journey from darkness to light can have many twists and turns. Sometimes we start out on foot but end up on wheels.

My journey one Sunday started poorly when I was not allowed to donate blood because my hemoglobin was too low. I like to give blood because it's a good gift that is easy to give. I always make sure I'm physically ready, and LeAnn helps by making sure I've had a good breakfast. But for whatever reason, I didn't make the grade so I walked off to Sunday school in a dark blue mood.

The blues continued when I sat down in the sanctuary to warm up with our wind ensemble and saw that the closing hymn for the service was "I Want to Walk as a Child of the Light." That was one of my late wife's favorite hymns and one I made sure we sang at her memorial service. That memory and rejection by the blood takers got me to thinking about how often she had to be poked and probed during her struggle with cancer.

I was still pondering that when it came time to sing the hymn, and then a glow of light came from the flute section. LeAnn, who knows what that hymn means to me, looked at me and mouthed, "Are you okay?" I nodded yes, and then joined with everyone in singing those simple, beautiful words:

In him there is no darkness at all;
The night and the day are both alike.
The Lamb is the light of the city of God.
Shine in my heart, Lord Jesus.[1]

I swallowed hard a couple of times, but I did not wallow in sadness. In fact, I felt like I crossed a threshold into some of that light.

That, in turn, prepared me to hear in a new way the family dedication that followed. When the pastor told the parents, "This little girl does not belong to you, she belongs to God, and she is a gift from God to you," I realized that those words are true about anyone we love. I looked over at LeAnn and saw just such a gift.

By the end of the day, I was reminded too that some of God's simple gifts come out of our silly disappointments. Had I been allowed to give blood, I might not have been in a reflective mood about all the bloodlettings of the past. I might have been too dull to be tweaked emotionally by that hymn, or to hear the family dedication with new ears. Most certainly, I'd have been in no physical shape to spend Sunday afternoon in such a wonderful way: on a long sunny bike ride with LeAnn.

Bravo! the Page Turners

It was a wonderful concert of violin and piano music, with a program that ranged from the eighteenth-century "Devil's Trill Sonata" by Giuseppe Tartini to John Williams' theme from "Schindler's List." In the intimate and acoustically superb setting of the choral hall, I not only could hear every note, but also I could see every stroke of the violinist's bow, every pressing of strings on the fingerboard, every movement of fingers on piano keys. And from where I sat, I also could see every movement of the pianist's page turner, and she, too, gave a remarkable performance.

The page tuner didn't play a note, but she saw and felt every note, watching the page as closely as the pianist and bobbing her head slightly with the tempo. And then at the right moment she'd stand up, lean over, pinch the corner of the next page, and when the pianist gave a little nod or made a murmur, she swiftly turned the page and smoothed it out as she sat back down to follow the notes to the next page turn. She was so immersed in the music that occasionally she would glance up at the violinist, her lips moving slightly as if humming the melody, and then she would close her eyes in anticipation of a moment of musical passion. That told me that she is more than just a page turner; she, too, is a musician—perhaps a violinist herself.

It was, I believe, a beautiful example of what we might call empathetic servant-hood. The page turner wasn't just "sitting in" and doing a job; she was feeling everything that the musicians were feeling because she knew the music by heart. And while she was contributing to their artistry—helping them move from measure to measure and page to page—she did so in a way that put herself in the background. This was their moment to shine.

Intrigued, I emailed the pianist, who I'd met just casually at church, and learned from him that the page turner is indeed an accomplished violinist and teacher in her own right. She plays in local symphonies and could easily be the star of the show, but she was no less the star by turning the pages. He said that before rehearsing with the violinist, he rehearses with the page turner. "After my music is learned, she generally helps us agree on tempos and transitions between sections. When we cannot come to terms on a difficult section (usually my fault), she generally has a safe solution. During concerts she is my safe zone. If I get lost, she always has a way of bringing us back together."

If the musicians got lost that night, it certainly wasn't evident to anyone listening. However, I think the audience got lost, applauding between the movements of a piece by Edvard Grieg instead of waiting silently until the end. Perhaps we lost our sense of decorum because we were lost in the beauty of the experience. But when the concert was over, we knew exactly what to do: we stood and applauded for all three artists—violinist, pianist, page turner.

Who do you know who is a page turner? Who turns your pages, keeps you on the right line, keeps you moving forward, helps you find your way when you get lost? Who works in the background so you can shine? Who is there with you through the allegros and adagios —the fleeting days and crawling hours—of your life? Who quietly experiences every moment alongside you? Who closes their eyes and prays with you and for you?

It might be a friend, a family member, a coworker, a neighbor. If someone comes to mind, send them a message of "Bravo!" in whatever way you can. Better yet, stand before them with an ovation of gratitude.

A Wonderful World?

Emotions were mixed on a Sunday evening as we listened to the Dallas Christian Jazz Band at a local club. As the big band played beautiful, lively arrangements of songs such as "Precious Lord, Take My Hand," the TVs on the walls flashed silently with a *60 Minutes* report on terrorist attacks in Paris. While my mind filled in the words to the melody—"through the storm, through the night, lead me on to the light"[2]—my eyes saw scenes of bodies draped with sheets on blood-stained streets.

Just a few hours earlier over Sunday lunch, a friend and I lamented our lack of understanding of God's justice in light of these events. Are we to wait for God's justice in God's way and in God's time and meanwhile take whatever harm may come? Are we to be instruments of God's justice and mount the attack to put an end to the terror? Or are we to try to reason with an ideology that is unreasonable?

Earlier that morning in church, I sat with the wind ensemble and played "Eternal Father, Strong to Save," with words that say:

O Trinity of love and power!
Our brethren shield in danger's hour;
From rock and tempest, fire and foe,
Protect them wheresoe'er they go.[3]

So where was that protection on the streets of Paris? And what do we do with Jesus' parable of the Good Samaritan, which was the focus of our gospel reading and sermon that morning? The story teaches us that our neighbor is not just the person we despise, but the person who feels that way about us. But Jesus doesn't tell us what to do when our neighbor wants to kill us on the streets of our cities.

Back at the concert, as the band played and the singer sang—"I see friends shaking hands, sayin', 'How do you do?' They're really sayin', 'I love you.'"[4] —the TVs flickered again with more images from France and a pre-game tribute at a professional football game to the fallen of Paris. It might have been a wonderful expression of support and unity, but in that moment I found it hard to think to myself, "what a wonderful world."

Finishing in Stride

For weeks before a backpack trip in the Utah wilderness with my brother and his sons, I went into training to make sure I was in good shape and wouldn't fall behind. I was motivated by a memory of when I was in Boy Scouts and one of the fathers on a week-long trek struggled much of the way. I didn't want to do that; I didn't want to be a burden and become a bad memory. I'm pleased to report that we had a wonderful trip and I came home invigorated and alive. However, I must confess that I did fall behind—not embarrassingly so, but behind just the same.

During four days covering about ten miles each day with backpacks of fifty-plus pounds, the five of us would start out together and over the next few hours the distance between us would grow. First in line was always the twenty-nine-year-old U.S. Marine, then alternately the fifteen- and twenty-four-year-old, and then my brother and me, fifty-eight and fifty-seven.

It would be easy to assume that my brother and I were always at the end of the line because we were thirty years older and less agile, but while the hike was demanding, the pace was not difficult. Every time we stopped for a break, my brother and I didn't come up huffing and puffing behind the others. We were not any more tired than the younger men.

But we discovered that at five foot ten and five foot eight, my brother and I were no match for his sons who are each six foot two. With longer legs, they easily covered more ground with each step. They weren't better hikers, and they weren't in better shape. They simply had longer strides. The only advantage for them was that they arrived a minute or so before us.

In camp, length of stride didn't matter. There, it was all about everyone contributing according to their ability and our common need. Each evening after we picked a campsite, everyone got busy: one went to get water, another dug a fire pit, others gathered wood and started the fire, and everyone pitched in to pitch tents. At mealtime we swapped and traded favorite foods, and on the trail we shared snacks and water. When the sole of my hiking boot began to fall apart, the Marine pulled out a roll of duct tape and patched me up. Later, when he needed a dab of sunscreen, I dug into my pack and made sure he was covered. Every night the younger guys stayed up a little later and put the last logs on the fire, and every morning the older men were up first to build a warming fire against the early chill.

In an age of "winner take all" on the one hand and "nobody should win" on the other, it's refreshing to walk on a middle ground where everyone works together so that all succeed at their own pace. It's done with patience, respect, fellowship, and love. It's not about being first or best. It's about being present for each other.

Floating Together

Water: it's a fundamental element of all life. We humans are approximately 60 percent water, which explains why we get thirsty and need to drink plenty of water to stay alive. Under the skin and down to the cellular level, every human being is made alive and kept alive by water.

We also are drawn to water for recreation. Whether it's a faraway memory of our dance in the womb or a cellular attraction to H_2O, we like to be near and in the water. This is especially true during the heat of summer, and especially with children. My parents have ancient home movies of us playing in the water—all spastic and jimmy-legged as we jumped through the spray of a lawn sprinkler and chased each other with the hose—and that hasn't changed with children.

In the water, children are equal. They play easily together and without prejudice; they all are there for nothing more than the refreshing splash of the water. We witnessed this while Ethan, our youngest nephew, was visiting us for a week one summer.

One afternoon we took him to the Legoland Discovery Center and ended the day at the center's splash park. We watched from the shade of an umbrella while kids of all ages and colors worked together under the spraying water to build a house out of large foam LEGOs. Ethan and another boy gathered bricks from all around and carried them in stacks to the construction site, where another group sorted through them and yet another built the walls. No one was more important than the other; no job was better than the other. There were no bosses or underlings—just everyone pitching in under the spray of the cool, refreshing water.

Later in the week, Ethan and I waded into the water at a wave pool where he and I were clearly the minority if you just considered skin color. But in the water, everyone was equal. The bell sounded and all the kids squealed with excitement as the waves began to come. They jumped on their floats and tubes and bobbed up and down in unison, bumping into each other without a care and enjoying the excitement of a day in the water.

That's the way it is with kids. They just don't seem to care about what divides them; they are only interested in what unites them, especially the water. But then something happens to them—to us. We grow up and get out of the water and forget our equality. In the white-hot heat of our personal aspirations and self-centered agendas, our skin becomes dry and rough, and our spirits do too. Before long we forget that we were equals back at the wave pool.

Worse than that, we forget that we are equals in the water of baptism. We also forget that those who have not yet found the saving waters are no less loved by God, and our own baptism calls us to share that love. At the wave pool the floats and tubes are shared; when kids get out for a while or leave, they push their floats over to those just arriving.

We seem to be living at a time when there is a great thirst for a better way. There is violence everywhere and little trust anywhere. You can almost hear society inhaling to let out a great, loud, collective wail—like a child left sitting alone in the sun, crying out for the cool of water.

I don't know what the solution is, but I do know that we have a choice to make: We can sink and drown under the weight of our fear and distrust, or we can accept our equal humanity, embrace our common baptism, and float on this sea of life together.

When it was time to leave the splash park, Ethan introduced us to Phil, his new friend. They wanted their picture taken together, and we took it. Ethan will never see Phil again, but when he sees the picture years from now, we hope he'll remember how two boys with different skin colors but kindred spirits played and worked together in the water.

Face to Face, Eye to Eye

Visiting a local Episcopal congregation to participate in a discussion about sharing faith through fiction writing, we were invited to stay for worship. It was a rich and warm experience. I especially liked the moment when the rector carried the gospel book from the altar down the aisle into the center of the church. Everyone was standing and turned to face her, which meant that as she read the day's gospel passage, we not only were seeing her but were also looking beyond her into the faces of one another.

I don't know the full meaning of this, but I found it to be a beautiful symbol of how God through Christ brought the word to us and we are invited to gather around it and live it in a personal way with each other. That idea was heightened by the gospel reading from Matthew 5:

> You are the light of the world. A town built on a hill cannot be hidden. Neither do people light a lamp and put it under a bowl. Instead they put it on its stand, and it gives light to everyone in the house. In the same way, let your light shine before others, that they may see your good deeds and glorify your Father in heaven. (v. 14)

As we heard the gospel, I could almost see the words of Jesus illuminated in the faces of those listening across from me.

Compare that with what I experienced a few days later at the county courts building. Sitting toward the back of the central jury room, I looked out across a sea of hundreds of fellow citizens, all facing forward—no eye contact, no visible expressions. We all had been summoned there to serve, but we were reticent, private, sleepy. We were hiding our lights.

That changed when they started calling jury pools and we were sent upstairs to wait outside our assigned courtrooms. There, sitting on church-like pews and facing each other, the darkness began to dissipate. People began to smile and to chat quietly as people do when bound together by a common experience.

The light began to shine more when we were called into the courtroom and one by one were asked questions—serious questions—that would help determine if we would be asked to serve. It was a DWI (driving while intoxicated) case, and potential jurors shared their personal stories of tragedy and weakness. In that room, there was no more hiding our light—especially as we faced the judge, lawyers, and defendant, and as they faced us. They were reading our light, and we were reading theirs.

I don't know if these two moments—one in church and the other at the court-house—have that much in common, but it does seem to me that we are better people when we live face to face, looking for the light in each other's eyes. I believe the gospel is stronger when we don't just read it but see others through it. And when we're called upon to judge our neighbors, it's good to do it face-to-face. We don't have to see the gospel light in their eyes. We just need to have that light in ours.

Valentines and Hellos

On Valentine's Day in grade school, we'd make mailboxes out of shoeboxes decorated with red construction paper, glitter, ribbons, and other arts and crafts stuff. Some years the mailboxes would sit on the corner of our desks, and other years we'd line them all up together on a shelf along the wall. At different times during the day we'd go around dropping Valentine's cards into each other's mailboxes, and at the end of the school day we'd have a party with cupcakes and punch, and we'd open our mailboxes to read the cards inside.

Most of the cards were store-bought, but some were homemade. Some were fun, some were serious, but what I remember most is that everyone got a card from everyone else. I don't know if it was school policy or simply a tradition, but it was a wonderful lesson that I remember more than any of the cards I received: Our class-mates were worthy of our love, and if not our love then our friendship, and if not our friendship then at the very least our acknowledgment.

Loving is easy because we choose who we love. Love is fun and exciting. Hating isn't fun, but it's equally easy. But acknowledging someone? That is so much harder. Acknowledging requires noticing. It requires risking a reaction. Acknowledging is nodding at someone waiting at a bus stop while you're waiting at a traffic light, saying hello to someone you pass in the grocery aisle, waving to a neighbor who steps out to check the mailbox at the same time as you, speaking to the clerk who checks you out at the store, staying on the sidewalk when someone approaches rather than crossing the street.

And yet, acknowledging may be vastly more important than loving someone. Acknowledging is that thin, fragile moment when a look or a gesture tells someone: "I see you. I notice you. I recognize that you and I are brothers or sisters, created by the same God and equally important and worthy of attention."

We know the Bible says, "Love your neighbor as yourself," but it's not talking about romantic, Valentine love. It's talking about acknowledgment. It's talking about seeing another person's humanity and giving that person courtesy and respect.

John Prine spoke of the power and importance of simple acknowledgment in a heartbreaking song called "Hello in There." The chorus and last verse go like this:

Ya' know that old trees just grow stronger,
And old rivers grow wilder every day.
Old people just grow lonesome
Waiting for someone to say, "Hello in there, hello."

So if you're walking down the street sometime
And spot some hollow ancient eyes,
Please don't just pass them by and stare
As if you didn't care, say, "Hello in there, hello."[5]

Valentine's Day comes once a year, but every day is a day to say, "Hello."

Appetite for Adventure

LeAnn and I got hooked on Food Network cooking competition shows one summer while on a business and vacation trip to Washington, D.C. The television in our hotel room was a mess at night. We couldn't find any shows we knew or wanted to watch, so we parked the TV on the Food Network.

One of our favorite shows on the Food Network is *Chopped*, where experienced chefs compete against each other to prepare appetizers, entrees, and desserts. Each course is a timed event, with losers "chopped" after each round. But the real fun is at the beginning of each round when the contestants open picnic baskets to reveal a surprising mix of ingredients they are required to use. Everyone has the same ingredients, but it is left up to them to decide what they do with the ingredients and what they add from a shared pantry.

Sometimes the mystery ingredients are truly strange. We've seen cotton candy, cow's tongue, dandelion greens, squid ink, lotus root, reindeer pâté—you get the idea. The chefs may scratch their heads for a moment, but then they rush around grabbing other ingredients and tools and after thirty minutes of chopping, mixing, baking, boiling, and every technique imaginable they create a dish that looks table-ready for a fine restaurant. Along the way they share pieces of their personal stories and what that brings to their dishes.

What intrigues me most is the depth of knowledge of the competing chefs. They have to know what flavors go together, the chemical interactions of fats and acids, cooking tolerances of different ingredients, and the pros and cons of frying vs. broiling vs. baking vs. boiling.

It's a lot like creating family or community. They're made of mixtures of personalities and talents—some familiar, some enjoyable, some peculiar, some irritating—and it takes some courage and basic knowledge of human nature to make them work. Even if you don't know what to do with the other people around the table, you at least should know how to handle yourself. That's a starting point for harmony rather than chaos.

On *Chopped*, the ingredients are chosen based on a foundational premise that every ingredient is redeemable and can contribute to something that is ultimately satisfying. It's the same around our table. Even the oddest among us are redeemable. We just have to use our patience and our spirit of adventure to figure it out.

More Than Words

At a memorial service I was attending, a man sitting in front of me reached into his suitcoat pocket and pulled out some paper. He unfolded it to reveal a program from another such service; I could see an oval portrait and the words "In Loving Memory" above it. He showed it to the person next to him and they both shook a little, apparently amused because he hadn't emptied his pocket since the last time he wore that suit.

I don't do much better. Sometimes I leave memorial service programs in the car door pocket for a day or two, or I place them on a corner of the kitchen counter or carry them up to my desk where I find them later. It just doesn't seem right to come home and throw the program in the recycling bin right away. After all, the obituary printed inside may be the last words written about that person.

They also may be the only words. As a rookie reporter at the Waco newspaper, I had to write police reports and obituaries. Although grunt work for sure, both were considered serious business, and obits were assigned with this stern warning: "For many people this is the only time they will ever get their name in the paper, so you better get it right."

I took that charge seriously, and it wasn't easy with the technology of the day. We didn't have email, so we took the information by phone or retyped it from forms delivered from the funeral homes. There were plenty of chances to make mistakes, but I must have done okay because I never heard otherwise. And along the way I gained a sense of who the people were—their accomplishments and the legacies and families they left behind. It was humbling work, but at age twenty-two I didn't spend a lot of time thinking about last words and legacies.

I've read a lot of obits since then in newspapers and memorial programs. I've helped write a few as a family member; I've read one over an open casket. They're all just words on paper, but they're not something to take lightly, and certainly they shouldn't be the last words written or spoken about a life.

If it's true that actions speak louder than words, then there are countless ways to actively honor and remember the ones we miss. I've done all the usual things: memorial donations, flowers at church on birthdays, adopting mannerisms and phrases. I've filled my days with mementos: Grandma's shelf clock announces the morning, LeAnn's father's cap protects me from the noontime sun, and Debra's lamp lights my book before going to sleep.

Better yet is to take the best of who someone was and live it forward. In my own way I've tried to share the optimism of Grandpa, the patience of Grandma, the strength of Grandad, the hospitality of Anna Belle, the laughter of Aunt Lucy, the peace of Uncle Kenny, the reverence of Dick, the faith of Debra, the enthusiasm of Perry, the friendliness of Paul.

It sounds a bit like *The Wizard of Oz*—courage, heart, brain, and all that—but we all embody these and other traits in different amounts depending on who has touched our lives. So let's not just remember them in words on paper or in silent thoughts; let's strive to share the best of their lives in the way we live with each other.

Running Wild

The sign stapled to the telephone pole had a picture of a little white dog, a phone number, and then these words: "Lost: Do Not Chase."

It seemed like a contradiction at first. If I see the little dog, shouldn't I snatch it up and call the number? Wouldn't that be the wise thing to do? Wouldn't calling the owner and saying, "I have your dog in my arms" be better than saying, "I saw your dog a while ago at the corner of Ninth and Avenue E"?

The answer is "no," because the owner obviously knows more about that dog than I do. It may be that the dog will run from strangers, or it will only be coaxed to safety by a certain treat, or it will come home when it's tired of running. The owner may know that the more you chase it, the more it will run away. If you chase it too much, it may get so frightened and frazzled that it will run blindly into the street, and then . . .

We had some experience with this when we first moved into our house. A little dog got loose, and eager to bond with our new neighbors, we joined the chase. But every time we got close to the dog it bolted—down the street, across a busy avenue, past the Baptist church and on to the Presbyterian church. And then it ran between some cars in a parking lot and seemed to just disappear completely. We looked around for a while and then gave up. The dog did go home to its owners, but only after the chase ended.

There are people in our lives like that. They are lost in whatever way they are lost—physically, spiritually, emotionally, and often a combination of these—and we want to bring them home where we believe they will be safe. But every time we reach for them, they jump away just out of our grasp. The more we chase them, the more reclusive they become. They don't answer their phone or email, they quit coming to church or the club, they start missing work, they hide behind their locked door.

Chasing them and risking them "running into traffic" seems like a bad option, but so does going about our business and hoping they'll come back on their own. My high school girlfriend broke up with me in a note that included that gem of 1970s' pop philosophy: "If you love someone, set them free. If they come back, they're yours; if they don't, they never were." Oh boohoo, that's not what we want to hear and that's not what we want to do.

I wonder sometimes if God looks at us this way. God knows we are lost, but instead of chasing us, God lets us run wild until we get tired and circle back toward home—like the father in the parable of the prodigal son. Or perhaps what seems like running away is God's plan for us running toward something new and good?

There's no question that God knows each of us better than anyone, and even better than we know ourselves, so it makes sense that God knows what will bring us back or push us forward to where we belong. And if the lost one is not us but someone we care for, that requires some prayerful discernment as to what our role should be.

I realize this is a serious topic for many people, and I don't take lightly that sometimes serious solutions are needed: intervention, counseling, medical attention, to name a few. But sometimes our role is to watch patiently from a safe distance and be ready to receive and welcome in whatever condition they are in.

If I see that little dog, I'm going to do what the sign says: I'll call that number, and I won't chase it. But maybe I'll keep watching from a distance and update the location if need be until the owner arrives and kneels down and that puppy jumps into her arms.

Lunch with a Stranger

We weren't looking for extra conversation—or advice, opinions, perspective, or anything else—but that's what Tom and I got one day.

I met Tom at a support group for widowers, and we sort of hit it off. I was ahead of him on the journey of grief and recovery and in fact was helping as a facilitator, but I gained fresh insight from hearing his story and renewed comfort in sharing mine. But then the group meetings ended, and we got busy and let too many months slip by without checking on each other. So, one day we made contact and planned to talk over lunch. The restaurant was crowded, and a man sat at a small table next to us with two plates of food and an apparent hunger for conversation.

"What brings you two here today?" he asked. I answered with a vague comment about "just getting together for lunch," and then I tried to continue my conversation with Tom. But the man was close enough to hear snippets of what we were talking about and he kept interjecting, although without the full context. When I asked Tom whether anyone had tried to set him up on a date—a serious question for a widower who is trying to ease back into a social life—the man interrupted by telling us how he had helped a forty-year-old friend start dating for the first time via an internet dating service.

Finally, when Tom got up to get a beverage refill, I told the man, "We both lost wives to cancer and we're just meeting for lunch to check on each other." I hoped that topic would scare him away, because frankly, it does scare most people away. Instead, it drew him in even further. "My wife is a six-year cancer survivor," he said, and over the next twenty minutes he shared details about that, his own serious health scares with heart attacks and diabetes, and his strong opinions about the state of health care in America.

Tom was a better sport about the intrusions than I, but he was the one who finally signaled it was time for us to leave. We talked some more in the parking lot and then shook hands and said goodbye.

The good thing that came from this is that the interruption prompted Tom and me to agree that we'd try not to let months go by before getting together again. But on top of that, we were reminded by our uninvited lunch guest that we live elbow-to-elbow with people who have survived crises and people who are still in the thick of crises. That's good reason to feel less alone, and even better reason to be more sensitive to strangers. You just never know what they're going through.

Going the Extra Miles

Years ago, my buddy Ken and I rode our bikes from Waco to Dallas. The total distance on the back roads of Central Texas was 124 miles. I think we did it in about twelve hours. This wasn't one of those big organized rides with aid stations and mobile mechanics and friends and families waiting at the finish line. This was just a couple of guys who wanted a good challenge on a hot summer Saturday.

Until that ride, the longest distance I'd cycled was thirty miles, and that was a reconnaissance trip for the big ride—to check out the route from the southern edge of Dallas County into the heart of the city and on northward to the suburbs.

I discovered in that experience that the only thing I needed to do differently from a physiological perspective to stretch myself from thirty to more than one hundred miles was to keep my body fueled. So, in addition to a lunch break at a café in Whitney, we drank plenty of water and ate fruit and energy snacks as we rolled. At the end of the 124-mile ride, I was no more tired than I had been after thirty miles.

However, there was one other factor that was crucial to survival and success: camaraderie with someone to help keep me going. When I made the thirty-mile ride, I was alone. It was a hard, stressful grind. I could never have done the longer ride by myself. I wouldn't have even tried.

In similar fashion, we've had eighty people at our house for a party but prior to that the most we had hosted was thirty. We weren't sure if we could do it on that large a scale, but once more the keys to success were plenty of good nourishment and camaraderie. In this case, I'll call it great fellowship—with all the guests but also with those who helped us prepare. We couldn't have done it alone.

There are so many things in life that seem daunting and even impossible on a large scale. However, if we have sufficient nourishment—be it physical, spiritual, or emotional—and if we have good folks with us to help carry the load and push us along, we can get through it. We can even enjoy it and make a great memory.

The bike ride was one of the best days of my life. I've added the house party to that list.

The Personal Touch

I've been writing a weekly blog for our church for a number of years, and as I begin to write each week I'm confronted and challenged by a message I've typed to myself at the top of the document that I always go to. I've even highlighted it in bright blue, so I won't miss it. The message is simple: KEEP IT PERSONAL.

The message is a reminder that when I share something from my own life rather than try to wax theological and sound like the seminarian that I am not, the message is better received. Readers have confirmed that with "likes" or comments, and even in the hallways at church. The latter is very satisfying because it is, well, personal.

I think that same message—keep it personal—if applied to almost any endeavor, will automatically improve the outcome. It definitely makes it more worthwhile and more memorable, and that often prompts a repeat. I learned that in a big way one summer when I volunteered to drive a large van on Wednesdays to a couple of retirement facilities and pick up a half dozen women for a noon meal and Bible study. And I learned it on the very first day.

I'd picked everyone up at the two locations, gotten them all buckled in and their walkers stowed, and rolled up to a major intersection where the van shuddered and then shut down. It was close to one hundred degrees outside, horribly humid, and the air conditioning had been running on high. There was no mistaking the problem: the battery had died.

Between calling the church for help, lowering the windows to get a breeze going, and jumping outside to wave the other cars around us, I fought back my panic and embarrassment. I also decided in my own mind that this was too much responsibility and I wouldn't subject myself to it again. Forget the personal touch of being a driver; I can help keep the buses running by writing a check.

But it didn't work out that way. The women calmed my fears by assuring me that they were okay and that everything was going to be fine. Help came, we got the bus started, and the women got to church on time. On the way back afterward, they were the ones apologizing to me for the inconvenience. All of them thanked me as they got off the bus, and I can still hear one of them saying, "We hope you weren't too discouraged. We hope you'll come back."

It was that message—their personal touch—that gave me the confidence to give it another try and to keep coming back for almost two years. A lot of what we do as a church or a community or a society does require financial support, but there's also a great need for people willing to help keep it personal.

Stepping Stones and Bridges

"Looks like we need to put down a stepping stone for the postman."

I said that one day after watching the postman jump over the peninsula of our flowerbed to cut across the lawn to the next house. Instead of walking down the front walk, he had made his own way and was determined to follow it, even when the zinnias had grown thigh high.

People will go where they need to go, and we can block them, we can live and let live, or we can try to make the way easier.

For a brief moment I had it in my mind to block the postman—to create a barrier that would force him back onto the sidewalk where I wanted him—but in the end that seemed heavy-handed and pointless. He wasn't really hurting anything, and who knows how many similar shortcuts he takes during the day that help him get to our mailbox and on through his route more quickly.

I was making that analysis in my head while sweeping the twigs, feathers, and dried bird droppings off the front porch. Earlier in the spring I pursued every imaginable strategy to keep doves from nesting in our hanging fern baskets. The doves responded by moving from basket to basket until they wore me down and I gave up. In the end they did no real harm, and in fact we got to witness the miracle of two hatchlings grow up under their mother's wings and fly away. Next year it will be live and let live.

Sometimes it is patient waiting that creates the best way to go. In writing an article about a new quadrangle on a college campus, I was intrigued to learn that grass would be planted but no sidewalks would be laid between the buildings initially. The landscape architect explained that many such places are crisscrossed with an ugly web of sidewalks—the ones designed by the planners, and the ones covering the ruts created by students. So, for this project they decided to wait and let the students' natural walking patterns determine where the sidewalks should be.

I was sweeping and thinking about all of that on the Saturday morning after spending several days at a denominational meeting in Dallas. The theme had been "Building Bridges," and the call was made to cross out of our comfort zones and go to people where they are, helping them and loving them in the context of their own cultures and experiences rather than dragging them over the bridges to our way of being.

It's a beautiful vision of ministry and mission, and yet the old mindset persists. On one afternoon, LeAnn and I were volunteering at the registration desk when I saw a woman in a saggy T-shirt and tattered shorts coming through the doors. Her face was sunburned and weathered, and she carried a large plastic bag seemingly bulging with everything she owned.

"Here comes a homeless woman," I whispered. And behind that whisper, I thought, "She doesn't belong here; this isn't for her."

But that is absurd; the work of the church is definitely for her, and she bravely crossed the bridge to come be with us. In fact, she told the volunteer at the next registration station that she was on her way to the Stew Pot community resource center when God told her to stop at the hotel and come inside. She didn't just belong there; she was invited.

The volunteer welcomed her, registered her, gave her a tote bag with all the usual stuff, and told her to have a great day. We didn't see her again. She might have attended a seminar or a worship service, or she might have just enjoyed a clean restroom and a cool place to rest for a while. Like the postman and the doves and the students crossing the quadrangle, she was free to choose her own path, and it was our duty and privilege to accept her as she was and help her if we could.

Later, riding home on a crowded commuter train after the last event, I watched in admiration as another one of our friends chatted with a young girl who had been to a museum with her father. Their talk was easy and fun, punctuated with smiles and laughter . . . two total strangers creating a brief bridge of friendship together—as natural as jumping over flowerbeds or meandering across a green quad.

Dirty Work

"Spread dirt." That's what it said on our calendar. LeAnn and I share our digital calendars to keep up with busy schedules and to make sure we don't drop an activity on top of something already there. It's not unusual for us to be miles apart and her phone or mine to buzz and we look down to see another item added to a busy week.

But this particular day was the day to "spread dirt," and it's something we planned and scheduled together. We were putting in new flowerbeds in the backyard. We'd been inspired by trips to gardens in Arkansas and Yosemite and especially Monet's garden in France. We want to fill the backyard with all manner of flowering plants that will come back year after year. We've also been inspired by author Robert Benson, who, in his book *Digging In*, documented what he called his "lawn-elimination project." His goal—and ours—is to spend less time mowing grass and more time smelling the roses and whatever else we can get to grow.

It takes lots of dirt for that, so we had three cubic yards of landscape mix dumped on our driveway that morning. We spent the afternoon shoveling it into a wheel barrel, dumping it in the new beds, and spreading it out. It's slow, repetitive work, and even on a cool day it makes the sweat run off my face. But it's good work because it's full of the hope and promise of new life and beautiful color.

The same can't be said for the other type of dirt-spreading going on all around us. It used to be that most of this dirt was just on the covers of the tabloids and magazines in the grocery store checkout lines. But dirt sells because people eat it up, and so it has jumped from the tabloids to the major newspapers and to the television news panels and late-night talk shows. And, of course, the dirt is distributed in dump truck loads by social media where sources and fact checks don't matter.

This dirt spreading is deadly. It buries the truth under lies; it suffocates hopes and dreams. It kills the spirit of the people being targeted and in time does the same to the dirt spreaders. And it's everywhere: in politics, in families, in churches, in schools, in businesses, in neighborhoods.

We had to make time on our calendar to spread our dirt, and it's amazing to me that people have time to spread so much of that other dirt. Are they not busy as we are with better things to do—feeding their families, paying their bills, helping their neighbors? Do they not enjoy the hope and promise of new life and beautiful color?

I suppose if they can make a living spreading dirt and it's easy to do—telling lies is always easier than telling the truth; spreading rumors is easier than checking facts—then the time-payback ratio is pretty good. But even so, have they no shame, have they no sense of decency? Aren't they tired of shoveling . . . dirt?

As I write this, I see Robert Benson's book on the shelf. I pray his flowerbeds are bringing up the beautiful blooms he envisioned and that we hope to have in God's good time. I pray, too, for a world that needs more color and beauty.

And Your Neighbor as Yourself

I don't have an answer to the violence in our world today. I have some opinions, but I don't dare voice them because every opinion I read is followed by a long chain of slap downs and insults and I don't want to contribute to that toxic mix. I have some ideas too, but ideas aren't well received nowadays either. Every one is angry.

More than angry, I'm disappointed and saddened by the current social environment in our nation. There are no verbal boundaries, no filters. Silence is no longer golden; loud and proud are the currencies of the day. This is not the country I was born into, but it is the country we have become. There are lots of reasons for that change, and the end result is ugly and sad.

It's hard to know what to do about it. It's easy to lob opinions into the bonfire and believe we've contributed. It's also easy to say, "I can't fix this," and do nothing at all. What's hard is to listen to one another and have civil conversations that lead to real solutions. We should all want an end to the violence. That, at the very least, should be a starting point—a place of common ground. The dreamer in me wants to believe that is true; the skeptic in me thinks there are profiteers out there stirring the pot.

I wish the solution was as easy as lighting candles, standing in circles, singing hymns, and raising prayers. I wish it was as easy as calling for a national day of prayer or lowering the flags for a week and only raising our heads and our flags again when everyone has agreed to be civil. But the finger-pointing and blame game always begin before the victims are even identified. The truth is we all are victims, and we all share the blame.

I wish I could open my Bible and find just the right verse that, if read out loud from the top of a tall building, would freeze everyone in their tracks and we all would be convicted and everything would change. I think I know what that verse would be:

"'Love the Lord your God with all your heart and with all your soul and with all your strength and with all your mind'; and, 'Love your neighbor as yourself'" (Luke 10:27).

Yes, I know I'm naïve. The solution seems so simple—just live those two verses, especially the second one—and yet it's probably impossible because too many people just don't seem to comprehend how precious and special is this one brief life that each of us has been given. There are moments when I can see it, feel it, taste it, and I know I'm part of something bigger than myself. But then there are moments when all I can see is my own reflection in the mirror and I forget that we are, each of us, equal in the eyes of God.

Get Real

Some friends gave us one of those smart speaker devices for Christmas, and I'll have to admit it was fascinating getting to know it and learning how it operates. It also focused a bright light on what is real and what is not.

Ours is a smart clock with a Google interface. It's not connected to any other devices or home systems such as the lights or HVAC, so we use it mostly for its primary purpose—a clock and alarm. But we also ask it for weather forecasts and quick fun facts. Sometimes it comes back with perfect answers, and sometimes it says, "I'm not sure how to answer that but my team and I are working on that." If we add a "please" to a request, it answers after first saying, "I like the way you asked that" or "I like hearing that magic word"—sort of reminds me of my grandmother.

At night we prompt the device for music to sleep by, and that has been the source of some frustration as well as humor. One time LeAnn said, "Play some old-fashioned love songs." She was thinking Frank Sinatra, Tony Bennett, Michael Bublé, Steve Tyrell. Instead, the device played "Right or Wrong," a high-energy western swing tune by Bob Wills and His Texas Playboys. LeAnn interrupted the music and said, "Play another song," and it jumped to "Take Me Back to Tulsa," another Bob Wills classic but definitely not something to sleep to.

So, just as the device is learning about us, we too are learning how to ask questions that make sense to the mysterious "team" at Google. "Old-fashioned" obviously means something different back at headquarters. On the other hand, the Google team must be steeped in paperback romance novels, because when I blurted for fun, "Hey Google . . . I love you man," the device answered back in its flat voice, "Thank you. I never thought this day would come. I like you too."

It's all good fun, but it's no replacement for real relationships and being hands-on and intentional about how you organize and live your life. One night over dessert with a friend we talked about how, in spite of these devices and social media, we are living in a world where people feel increasingly lonely and isolated. She paraphrased the author of a book she had read or a speaker she had heard who commented that Twitter can't visit you when you are lonely, and Facebook can't sit by your bedside when you are sick or dying. And yet we are spending more and more of our time with our faces buried in our screens.

Every Sunday morning, my iPad and my iPhone automatically give me an update on the past week's screen time. It's sobering when it shows a percentage increase, especially when that is stacked on top of a previous week's increase. It's also ironic that the update comes while I'm at church. I'm sitting in Bible study or worship—presumably giving God my time and attention—when my pocket buzzes, and like Pavlov's dog I pull out my phone to check it. Ninety-nine times out of a hundred, instead of it being something urgent that needs my attention, it's just another wasted moment that will add to the new week's percentage of screen time.

God gave us minds to invent and build these devices. They can be and often are amazing tools for good—for teaching, for learning, for setting priorities, and keeping calendars. We've seen amazing moments when swarms of people have been mobilized by social media to rise up and help right a social wrong. And social media powered by hand-held devices has launched revolutions and saved lives in the face of natural disasters. But the hallmark of those events was that real people got out and did the real work of helping each other.

With that in mind, I asked our smart clock, "How can I help people today?" It gave me a short list from a Zen-focused website of ways to affirm people and show appreciation, and then it suggested I clean out the pantry or buy a bag of groceries to donate to a homeless shelter. That's right on target; that's real. But when I asked, "Would you like to go out and help me do that?" the response was, "I'm sorry, I don't know how to answer that question."

Centered

One night at our church wind ensemble rehearsal, we were practicing a piece called "Consolation" by Noah D. Taylor, when our director stopped us and suggested we try something new: spread out in a large circle and play the piece while facing each other. She said it would help us hear who has the most important parts at different times, especially as the dynamics—the loudness and softness—change, and it would help us play more in tune.

So, we picked up our music stands and instruments and spread out into a large circle that rose and fell with the contours of the risers in the choral hall. We didn't move our chairs; we all stood, looking more like a jazz band than a wind ensemble, and we played through the piece.

As the name "Consolation" hints, the piece is thoughtful and emotional. To quote from publisher J.W. Pepper, it "passionately evokes the emotions one endures when they find a source of comfort in a time of suffering or grief. Representing the complex emotions of the human condition, are juxtapositioned moments of quiet solace, building tension, and immense emotional release."

When we finished playing, our director asked, "Did you hear it?" and the answer was, "Yes." Facing each other, we could hear each other's parts better than we do when facing the back of the person in front of us. And hearing all the parts better, we ebbed and flowed better together, and we played more in tune. Someone noted that standing had a way of opening up the airways and enhancing our breathing that we don't experience when slumped in a chair. For me, standing with the weight of a fifteen-pound baritone saxophone hanging from my neck sharpened my focus and attention.

I've played standing and facing one another in a small quartet, but I've never done that before with a large group. I have to admit the experience and the sound was remarkable. We haven't taken that on as a regular way to rehearse, and we certainly won't arrange ourselves that way in worship. But it served a valuable purpose in the way it changed our focus from just the music on our stands to the music coming from each other and being created together.

In that way it's an example of how community should be and can be—where people are facing each other, working together, listening to each other, respecting each other's efforts and contributions. As members of communities—and we all are whether it be family, civic, business, cultural, or spiritual—are we not better able to provide comfort and consolation when we are facing each other than when we are looking outward and away?

Perhaps this is something to work on: to turn toward the center, to listen for balance and harmony, and to rediscover how our life fits with Christ's and with each other's. Because when we put Christ in the center and face the center, we also find that we are looking through Him toward each other.

Trending

For a long time now I've been unpacking and tweaking an idea that I thought I would drop sometime soon. My goal was that if it resonated and went viral or at least trended, I might get some traction and maybe crush the conversation and grow my platform. But it wasn't in my wheelhouse and in fact was above my pay grade, so I decided to shelve it. I didn't want an epic fail that would get trolled and shaded with LOL or SMH and especially not LMAO.

Did reading that paragraph sort of make you sick to your stomach? I got nauseous writing it. That's the language we speak today; that's the world we live in now. Everyone's working hard to out-do, one-up, and best each other with click bait to blow up the internet. And what's the prize? A rush of likes, friends, and followers, usually for just a few minutes before the shamers jump in and drag you down into the digital gutter.

I don't know if it's solely technology driven or the sad, soulless evolution of our language and our sensibility. It may be both, but it's everywhere and it's making us sick—more so than climate change, politics, guns, violence, disease, hunger, and all the ills of the world combined. It takes those serious problems that need real solutions and squeezes them down into topics to be debated and spun with 120 characters or fewer. Finding solutions is less important than generating clicks. Short of the internet going dark forever, I don't see any way out but one: "Love the Lord your God with all your heart, and with all your soul, and with all your mind . . . and love your neighbor as yourself."

It's not a bombshell; it's a whisper. In this graceless, cutthroat age it reads like a cutesy slogan painted on a slab of wood at an antique mall. It's milquetoast in the land of avenging superheroes. It's too simple to be taken seriously. Really, we can change the tone and change the world with love for God and each other? Cue the laughing yellow emojis and the "no way" gifs.

Go ahead and shame me and shade me if you wish, but this simple statement of love has been trending quietly for thousands of years—not just the words but the actions they generate. We see little examples every now and then on the late news. We've even seen waves at different times in history. But it's never been tried by all of humanity at the same time.

I wish it would go viral, but God doesn't seem to work that way.

CHURCH AND THE KINGDOM: KINDRED SPIRITS

My earliest memories have flashes of the sights and sounds of church. I was raised in the church, and it's been my second home my entire life. But as I've grown older, the walls of the church have fallen away with the understanding that the church is the people and not the buildings or the place. What's more, the church is not just those who share my faith traditions, but it encompasses all believers.

Like the human family, the spiritual community claims everyone who has ever lived. Whether or not we go to church or even declare a faith, we all are spiritual beings fashioned by a divine creator. The question is: How do we embrace our place in this community—if we embrace it at all?

Flat Wooden People

Before knowing LeAnn and entering her world of early childhood education, there was a room at our church I didn't know existed: the preschool resource room. It's where all the goodies are stored for the Sunday and weekday preschool and children's classes.

From floor to ceiling, the resource room is organized with bins holding everything needed to stimulate young minds: colored paper, fuzzy pipe cleaners, Play-Doh, paint and brushes, toy trucks and airplanes, puzzles, drums and rhythm sticks, blocks and balls, magnetic letters and numbers, glitter and bric-a-brac, and odds and ends that only children know how to transform into temples, chariots, and scrolls.

I was in the resource room early one Sunday morning helping LeAnn gather materials for Sunday School and came upon a bin labeled, "Flat Wooden People." Looking inside, I found exactly what the label said: flat wooden cutouts of people. I assume they are used for role-playing lessons, but my grown-up mind went somewhere else.

Too often, we Christians are looked upon as flat wooden people. It's a stereotype that comes from certain groups of us who equate righteous living with humorless living—who tamp down smiles and laughter in favor of a strict and stern demeanor. It also comes from those who point bony fingers of judgment at people who don't act and behave exactly as they do. That sometimes includes those who don't worship and pray the way they do.

The stereotype leads to comments such as, "Oh, you're one of *those* people," when you try to help someone or share your faith. It also leads to charges of hypocrisy when you fail to match the stereotype to the letter. Worst of all, it leads people to think they don't belong in church because their lives are too messy; they aren't buttoned down enough.

Throughout his ministry, Jesus fought against these flat wooden stereotypes. He dared to throw open the doors of the kingdom of God to everyone—especially flawed, hurting, flesh-and-blood people. And he dared to throw out the rulebooks that measured holiness by a strict lifestyle and focused instead on relationships that bring a rich, joyful style to life.

The truth is that the least flat, most three-dimensional people I know are Christians. They like to laugh, they like to work hard and play hard, and they find Sundays at church to be a highlight of the week. That doesn't mean they aren't reverent, or that they don't share serious moments. It means they help each other get through those moments and figure out how to smile again—often with humor that pokes fun at themselves.

That type of joyful Christianity should be taught early at church—so early that the only flat wooden people to be found are stowed back in their bin at the end of Sunday school.

Keep Your Head On

I laughed out loud when I read a former child star's description of growing up on the set of *The New Mickey Mouse Club*. He said: "Backstage at Disney World, there are stories. Mickey Mouse with his head off, drinking coffee on break. Pirates on the phone. Ghosts in line for food."

I had the same feeling as a kid when I saw Jerry Haynes—"Mr. Peppermint" on our local kids' TV show—out of his signature red-and-white-striped jacket shopping at the mall or eating at a restaurant. Years later when Haynes passed away, I was reminded that the people we idolize or revere at different times in our lives are, in the end, just flesh-and-blood humans. Take off their costume and they eat and drink, laugh and cry, live and die, just like the rest of us. It's in those unguarded moments off the stage when a person's true character is in the spotlight. Reading Haynes's obituary, it was clear that he was the same decent, generous man with or without the candy-striped costume.

So it is for us outside of the church and out in the community where we can behave—or misbehave—just like everyone else. I'll admit that for the most part, my childhood in the church has influenced my actions outside the church. I'll also admit that there have been plenty of times when I've totally forgotten who I am and where I am and have behaved in a way that would embarrass my pastor, Sunday school teachers, parents, and friends—not to mention disappoint God.

The Gospels and Paul's letters to the early church have plenty to say about the dangers of hypocrisy, bearing false witness, and being a stumbling block to the faith of others. The notion of "sinner on Saturday, saved on Sunday" was as prevalent then as it is today.

Paul wrote of a "thorn in the flesh"—an unspecified weakness—that kept him from being conceited because it was only through God's power that he could overcome it. My biggest weakness is impatience, which itself is a form of conceit. It looks like irritation or frustration, but the underlying feeling is superiority: "I'm more intelligent, my way is best, my time is more important." It's the reason people honk their horns, bark at waiters, and huff and puff when the checkout line is moving slowly.

So how do we keep from losing our heads when we take off the costume of a Sunday saint? The simple answer is that we keep the costume on and grow into it until it is no longer a costume but who we really are. The more human answer is that we just keep working at it and remain mindful of our own failings. And we do as Paul suggests and lean on God's strength to overcome our weaknesses

Keeping Up with the Family

"Looks like most of the family is here!" That was the enthusiastic observation from the thirtyish young man who settled in behind us in the metal bleachers at a college football game one Saturday evening. "I mean, as season ticket holders we're sort of like family here, right?" he added.

This was my first experience with season tickets of any type, and after a few games I understood what he was saying. Beside us, behind us, and in front of us were individuals and groups who were in the same location week after week. To my right and in front of me were LeAnn and some of her long-time friends who have been true "family" to her over the years and who have adopted me as well. The rest are strangers—but familiar strangers just the same.

Behind us was the young man and his friends who we enjoyed because of their energy and wisecracks about the games. To my immediate left was a family with a teenage boy who during every game would eat everything on the concession stand menu board. And radiating out were others whose names we didn't know, but we recognized them, said hello and goodbye, shared high-fives when something great happened, and joined in a collective groan when things went bad. When one of these folks was absent, we took notice and even worried a little.

One year our church started a "pew shepherd" program that asked members who sit in the same vicinity each week (isn't that everyone?!) to keep a caring eye out for their neighbors—to greet guests in their midst, but also check on regulars who might be missing. It's a great idea and a wonderful way to build "family."

One of the prime reasons I joined my church years ago was because I was treated like family right away. I had visited a few times, and one Sunday when the head usher needed someone to help collect the offering, he recognized me and put his trust in me. "But I'm not a member," I said. "Doesn't matter. I need you," he replied.

Contrast that to me running into a church member downtown who I hadn't seen in a long time. When I asked, "Where have you been?" she replied, "I had to be away for a while, and when nobody checked on me, I figured that I wasn't really missed." She quit coming, and I was among those who carelessly let that happen.

That's not the way to be a family—whether connected by faith, blood, or school colors.

Building a Community with Heart

"Kneeling with our fallen brethren; Pressing, breathing life anew . . ." Sounds like the words to a hymn, but it's actually my own two-line summary of two hours of instruction in CPR (cardiopulmonary resuscitation) that twenty of us received on a Sunday afternoon at church. I'm heartened to know there are people among us who are trained to give this life-saving aid.

While our parish nurse was putting us through the paces with plastic CPR dummies, another group down the hall was brainstorming the future of the church. From what I heard later, the concept of "community" was a focus of that discussion. Specifically, "What can we do to build a true community of faith?"

I believe one of the things we can do to achieve that is to practice another type of CPR: compassionate personal response. There are many ways churches are doing this already by training laypeople for various ministries, but all of us are capable of providing compassionate personal response at different levels. And I think there are parallels to the key steps of cardiopulmonary resuscitation.

1. Make sure the area is safe.
That one should be easy because the church should be a safe place, and church people should be trusted with our pain and distress.

2. Tap and shout, "Are you okay?"
Community is a two-way street, and this is where things can break down. We're usually comfortable sharing our physical ailments, but we're not so open about our spiritual and emotional pain. No one really wants to admit they're hurting or broken. We want to appear buttoned down and together, and when some one asks, "How are you doing?" it's easy to stoically reply, "Fine," even if we're not. If we truly want and

need help—and if we want to build true community—we need to be more honest with ourselves and with each other.

3. Yell for help. Send someone to phone 911, and get an automated external defibrillator.
We're not all equipped to handle complicated situations. Thankfully, the church is peopled with professionals at every level: pastoral counselors, psychologists, medical doctors, Stephen ministers, care teams. If you're in over your head, or you're uncertain about the situation, you don't have to go it alone.

4. With the heel of your hand on the breastbone, compress the chest hard and quickly thirty times, then stop and give two quick breaths.
This is where both types of CPR get risky. With cardiopulmonary resuscitation, it's possible to break someone's ribs, bruise them, or expose them to embarrassment by opening their shirt. The same is true with compassionate personal response: We can cause discomfort and embarrassment by asking questions. But as our nurse said, it is better to risk injury and embarrassment and save a life than to do nothing and lose a life.

5. Trust your instincts.
This is not one of the actual steps of CPR, but it is something our nurse emphasized during our class. She said that in a real emergency, our mental recall will kick in and we'll know what to do. I believe the same is true when being "community" with each other. And with both types of CPR, we can go a step further and trust God with the results.

Instruments of Discovery

One Sunday morning, while most of the grown-ups were sitting in the sanctuary learning about parables, I was sitting in a grown-up's chair in the kindergarten Sunday school department. The children were learning about how Solomon obeyed God, built the temple, and celebrated with prayer, songs, and the playing of instruments. I was there at LeAnn's invitation to illustrate the instruments part of the story.

Before I opened my large black instrument case, the children were asked to guess what was in it, and the answers included a guitar, a trombone, and even a piano. When I opened the lid and pulled out the bright brass baritone saxophone, there were gasps and immediate requests to touch it. They got to do that, but first I played the lowest note I could, and then the highest, and then a scale from bottom to top and back again. And then I played "Jesus Loves Me This I Know" with the children singing along.

It was fun, but I have to admit I wasn't keen on the gig at first. I have a lifelong aversion to speaking, singing, playing, or doing anything solo in public, and it doesn't matter if the audience is preschoolers or corporate executives. In fact, I made that point at the first meeting of an adult education committee earlier in the year. When we went around the room to introduce ourselves and various people mentioned their teaching backgrounds, I bluntly said, "I've never taught a class, and you shouldn't want me to teach a class because I can hardly speak in public."

But on this Sunday with the children, somewhere between low A and high F-sharp I had a flickering memory of sitting in a Sunday school room when I was a child and watching a man play a long brown bassoon. I recalled feeling some fascination with the mechanics of the silver keys pressed by the man's hands to produce different sounds. I joined the school band in sixth grade and played through freshman year in college and then took a twenty-five-year break before coming back to music and playing with the church wind ensemble.

It's possible that all of that occurred because a man took the time to play a few notes on the bassoon for a bunch of squirmy kids. And maybe my five minutes of discomfort helped start one of these kids on the path to music. Perhaps you can do the same thing by sharing a hobby, talent, or skill—something you love to do. It's worth the effort because we never know when we're being instruments of discovery.

In Unison

During the memorial service for a longtime, beloved minister of music, we recited the 23rd Psalm, and while the order of worship said, "Unison Reading," for a brief phrase or two the sound was anything but that. Like joggers starting a run together, we started at different paces.

A tall man with a strong voice sitting close to me pulled out in front and headed for "green pastures" while some of us still were making the turn at "I shall not want." But then, as if looking over his shoulder, the man slowed down a little and let us catch up. By the time we reached "the valley," we all indeed were speaking in unison and arrived at "the house of the Lord" at the same time, together.

That is the joy and miracle of being church—whether the church in the world at large or a single congregation. If we're listening to each other and watching each other, we start to move as one body, and preferably the body of Christ. It can happen when we recite a psalm or the Lord's Prayer. It also can happen when we plan ministries, go on mission, or make decisions together.

All it takes are ears for attentive listening, mouths for honest sharing, heads for faithful discerning, and hearts for trusting God and each other.

What's Bugging You?

"Were there bed bugs at Pentecost?"

The question came from a child in the kindergarten Sunday school class who had been paying close attention. She'd heard from her parents that in places where lots of travelers gather, such as New York City, there are bed bugs. So, when she heard in Sunday school that thousands of people traveled to Jerusalem for Pentecost, the question made perfect sense. The answer from LeAnn, her teacher, was simple and straightforward: "We just don't know."

What we do know about bed bugs is that they don't differentiate between income or social status. They can invade everything from apartments and small houses to mansions and posh hotels. They travel with ease in the clothing and luggage of their hosts, so it's definitely possible that the people gathered in Jerusalem for Pentecost were susceptible to infestation. We don't know for sure because, with the exception of a few stories such as the plague of locusts that God put on Egypt, the Bible is not an entomological study.

What we do know about Pentecost is that the Holy Spirit descended on people of all nationalities, races, and cultures. The Holy Spirit did not come just for the wealthy or the influential but for everyone, so that all might have an intimate relationship with God. Just as bed bugs might be found on Park Avenue or Skid Row, in an upper room or inside the Temple, so the Holy Spirit is found everywhere.

And what does the Holy Spirit do? You had to see the pun coming: it bugs us . . . in a good way, of course. It gives us an itch to pursue a Christ-centered life. It reminds us of who we are and whose we are. It provides comfort when we're broken and hurting. And when we get off into the tall grass of our own ambitions and appetites, it makes us uncomfortable and even keeps us up at night.

So, what's bugging you? How is the Holy Spirit keeping you up at night? Are you feeling the Holy Spirit pulling you toward a new ministry or a career change that will lead you from a job to a vocation?

I got that itch some years ago. And while the way has seemed uncertain at times, it's always been fulfilling and meaningful. After almost three decades of preparation, I felt as if God had finally matched my God-given talents with a God-given calling.

Perhaps you feel the urge to pursue a new relationship or rekindle one that has been lost or soured. I lost touch with my best friend for almost ten years out of busyness and neglect, and when we finally reconnected, we said, "Never again," because we'd forgotten how much we love and need each other. As it happened, we reconnected at a time when we both needed the support of someone who knew us well. Indeed, the Holy Spirit was at work.

Maybe you've collected some baggage—bad habits, poor choices—that you need to carry to the dump and leave behind. I know that sounds like a New Year's resolution and not something you would normally consider at Pentecost or any other time of the year, but when the Holy Spirit starts chewing on you, the only way to stop the rash is to pay attention and take action.

Breathless

Staggered breathing: that's what musicians in a section who are playing or singing the same part do when they need to take a breath but don't want to create a gap in the music by everyone inhaling at the same time. By alternating their breaths, they create a seamless note or phrase.

The technique took a profound turn once at the conclusion of a rehearsal for our church wind ensemble. We ended the hour as we always do by sharing concerns, and then someone was asked to pray. But a few sentences into the prayer, the person praying was overcome by emotion and gently nudged the adjacent player in that section. That person continued the prayer immediately and carried it all the way to "amen." The result was a continuous, seamless prayer.

We'll call it staggered praying, and that's what we can do when we pray with each other. Instead of letting someone get fatigued or distracted or overcome, we can continue a thought and even expand on it to create a continuous flow of petition, thanksgiving, blessing, or whatever the focus of the prayer time is.

There come times in most of our lives when we've prayed about something so long and so hard that we've run out of words and we're prayed out. That's a good time to have someone close by who we can nudge to continue the prayer on our behalf. In that way, we can help each other "pray without ceasing," as Paul said (1 Thess. 5:17).

With staggered breathing, the more people you have playing in a section, the less winded they become and the better they are able to perform. The flutes, clarinets, and trumpets often benefit the most because those are the biggest sections. Playing the baritone saxophone, I've rarely had a section mate, but I often have the same melody or harmony lines as the euphoniums, trombones, or tubas, so I try to stagger my breathing with them. Since we don't sit together, I do it without them knowing it. Similarly, we can stagger our prayers with those in need without them ever knowing it. That's what prayer lists are all about.

Immediately after the final "amen" of the staggered prayer I described, someone else in the band said, "Now that's a section!" When we pray together that way in church, it might be said, "Now that's a church!"

Service with a Smile

Sometimes you can try so hard to do something right that you risk crushing the entire effort. That's what I learned when asked to coordinate the ushers and offering collectors for a denominational convention.

I'll start by admitting that I overplanned with hopes of getting everything just right. Armed with a seating chart for the assembly hall, a list of volunteers for each of the five sessions, and instructions for what we were to do at each session, I spent several hours in the days before the meetings plotting exactly where and how each person would serve. Understand that most of the volunteers were people I had never met before, so it seemed like a good idea to organize everything on paper.

All the planning was for naught. When I entered the main assembly hall early before the first session, I found that two large sections of seating had been eliminated, rendering my carefully labeled charts obsolete. On top of that, some of our duties changed before we even got started, and the volunteer mix was in flux—as often happens when people have last-minute conflicts.

But then something interesting happened. As I stood over a table in a small meeting room, trying to rearrange everything on paper, I glanced up and saw one of the volunteers smiling patiently at me. Others were talking and laughing among themselves, and that's when I knew it was time to put away the charts. We all walked over to the assembly hall and the volunteers naturally paired up and chose the sections they wanted to serve. The three sessions that day proceeded without a hitch.

I had a new crew the next day, and I told them our main objective for the morning business session was to prepare ballots to distribute quickly to every person in the hall. But then I added that the ballots are rarely needed and probably won't be needed this time, but we still had to be ready. So, everyone jumped in and began counting out stacks of ballots for each row, talking and visiting all the while. No one said, "This is silly" or, "This is a waste of time." They did the work willingly, and later in the morning when the ballots weren't needed, they helped box them up for the following year.

Evening worship was very busy for us with an offering to collect, a Communion service to help guide folks through, and a special brochure to distribute. I was worried when we had more ushers than we needed, but some gave up or shared tasks so that everyone could experience the joy of serving.

The lesson I learned in all of this is that truly cheerful servants roll with the punches, go with the flow, bend with the wind, rise and fall with the tide. They're not worried about perfect plans, clean divisions of duty, clear lines of command. They just want to be in on the action, to be there on the scene, working shoulder-to-shoulder with each other. Perfect results are not the goal; completing the mission is what matters, even if the mission changes.

Running with the Saints

It is a rite of early August at our house each year: a strung-out, raggedy line of high school girls running down our street. Actually, some are running and some are stopping and bending over to catch their breath. Driving alongside them is their coach. If she sees us standing on the porch, she might shout from her open windows, "This year's cross-country team," and we might answer back with a "good luck" and a thumbs up.

Good luck indeed, because in August these are not the muscular, toned, confident young women from the high school who one May chose our front porch to pose for a picture as the state championship track team. Maybe in ten months some of the August girls will be ready for that photo. In the future, one or more of them may stand on a podium at an NCAA meet, or the national championships, or even the Olympics. But on those early mornings in August, many are just struggling to stand at all.

I never ran track in school, but I was in marching band, so I know a lot needs to happen before any medals or trophies can be claimed. First, there will have to be practice, practice, practice until the weak become strong and the timid become confident. Along the way, the strong will have to become leaders, and the leaders will need to become selfless and humble if they are going to have a winning team.

That last part may be the most difficult, because our human tendency is to keep running and not look back once we get out in front. But as we often see in the Olympics—where the top gymnasts need the talents of their teammates to help them win a medal—even the strongest need help.

It's true in athletics, it's true in business, it's true in life, and it's true in the church: At some time or another each of us will need help from someone else to get up on our feet and start running again.

It's that humanity that keeps many Christian denominations from formally singling out people as "saints" the same way we induct athletes into halls of fame. By avoiding that practice, we acknowledge that each of us is prone to stumble and fall, and yet we're also imbued with the Holy Spirit and are capable of leading and serving in important ways—some that will get noticed, and some that won't.

That leaves room for both canonized "Saints" and beloved "saints." And it leaves room for the high schooler I saw one morning who slowed down a little, turned and shouted, "Come on, Becky!"

Called by Name

"Florida Stranger." That's the name I had in the contacts list on my cell phone for a woman in Florida who called me more than a dozen times over a few months one year. When I first answered the phone, she said she had misdialed. The second time, she apologized and said she had reversed the last four numbers. Third time, same thing. Sensing that the errant calls would continue, I created the contact name for her so I would see it and ignore it in the future.

The problem with that is once you give something or someone a name, they gain a personality and you no longer feel comfortable ignoring them. That happened with "Florida Stranger." The very next time she called I felt bad about ignoring her and I answered. We chatted a moment. She apologized again and said she'd try to stop making that mistake. I wished her luck and a good day. The calls kept coming and I finally gained some backbone and quit answering, but each time I saw her name I felt like I was ignoring someone I knew.

In the 1980s, I met a homeless man downtown, and when he asked my name, common courtesy required that I return the favor and ask his. For the next couple of years, Dane and I had an ongoing relationship in which I tried to offer him friendship and a little help here and there. Sometimes it was fulfilling and sometimes it was aggravating, but I couldn't ignore him because I knew him by name.

When we moved to a new neighborhood, we got to know many of our new neighbors by name, and that led to waving and "hellos" and helping each other in little ways such as digging holes and chasing dogs. One time when we went to a "Shakespeare in the Park" performance, I ran into one of these folks in the crowd and we simultaneously called each other by name.

The same thing can and should happen at church. Our church is big compared to some churches, and small compared to others, but there are some among us who make sure no one is ignored in the crowd. Our greeters do a wonderful job of this at the doors on Sunday mornings. And anyone who has sat down in the sanctuary a half hour before the service begins has seen some early arrivers who go up and down the aisles, greeting members and guests alike, asking their names. It's their ministry and gift to make sure no one is anonymous in God's house.

That's important because none of us is anonymous in God's eyes. Through the Scriptures we see numerous times how God called people by name—Samuel, Moses, Jacob, Jonah, David, Israel—and made the relationship personal. In Isaiah we read: "I have redeemed you; I have summoned you by name; you are mine" (43:1). Those words became flesh in the New Testament with Jesus calling his disciples, his followers, and even those that official religion had ignored into a personal relationship.

Just as we each are called, we can help call others into the community of faith by first calling them by name.

Singing by Heart

As the bright, familiar guitar intro to Van Morrison's "Brown Eyed Girl" came across the speakers at the deli, I looked up from my plate to see two men bobbing their heads. One was sitting at a table with his teenage daughter, and the other was waiting for a to-go order. As Morrison began to sing, so did they: "Hey where did we go, days when the rains came . . ."[1]

I was asking myself that same question—"Hey where did we go?"—the previous night at a college football game when the halftime announcer said the marching band would be playing Billboard Top 40 hits of the past decade. I didn't know the songs at all, and when one was introduced as a "smash hit," I grumbled aloud that I'd never heard of the song or the artist. LeAnn explained: "That's because we're old."

No wonder that I felt redeemed at the deli the next day. I felt I belonged because I knew the song.

Popular culture divides us by age, gender, race, size, education, geography—every imaginable category. Sometimes it can turn groups against each other, and at the least it can leave us asking ourselves, "Hey, where did we go?"

Our faith, on the other hand, can erase the lines that divide us. It can draw us together to a common God and a shared future in Christ. I experienced a piece of that on a Sunday morning as I sat on the floor with three-year-olds to listen to a teacher read a picture book with snippets from the biblical stories of Adam, Noah, Moses, Samson, Joseph, Ruth, John, and Jesus. Already, the children were raising their hands as they recognized pieces of stories that I've known for years. It's like we knew the same song, just at different levels of understanding.

In a larger way, our church sings in unison with churches around the world. While we are Baptists and have the freedom to shape our own worship experience, we often follow the lectionary of the church universal. That puts us in tune with millions of Christians around the world. Just imagine: On any given Sunday, more of us are tuned into the same Scripture than the number of people watching the all-time highest-rated television programs: Super Bowls, Oscars, royal weddings, World Cup championships. In other words, we are never more united—and we never belong together more—than we do when we worship the same Lord.

Sadly, we're never more divided than when we fight over the same Lord, creating divisions that are more dangerous than any created by popular or secular culture. Christians, Jews, and Muslims should be singing the praises of the one true God instead of bludgeoning each other with intolerance fueled by pride, greed, ignorance, and fear. We Christians might lead the way, but even we are on different pages of the hymnal sometimes.

Holy Voice

Once a month I would meet my friend Paul downtown for lunch, but we always started at the Catholic cathedral where Paul read the Scripture during the noon mass. I usually got there ten or fifteen minutes early and enjoyed sitting in the large, dark sanctuary to pray, think, or just experience the quiet.

On one visit the quiet was interrupted by a toddler, standing on the pew next to his kneeling mother, making popping noises and short shouts. As he did so, he twisted his body to look up at the ceiling, apparently intrigued by the echo of his own voice.

On a Sunday not long after that, Peter Marty, pastor and publisher of *The Christian Century*, spoke to a luncheon group at our church about hospitality. When asked to critique what he observed at our church, he said he would like to see more small children in the worship service. He reasoned that even if children don't understand the hymns, Scriptures, prayers, and sermons, they begin to experience the sights and sounds of church, and that begins to become a part of who they are.

I suspect many churches keep children out of "big church" until they reach an age of understanding and discipline precisely to prevent the disruptive behavior that I witnessed at the cathedral. I do understand that, and I respect the expertise of child development experts and parents who know more about this than me.

Still, I'm intrigued by Marty's perspective. I wonder if what I witnessed at the cathedral was a little boy's first rough attempt at prayers—sending his voice upward and hearing it echo back. Perhaps someday he'll be there as his mother was, praying and listening for the response of the Holy Spirit.

And, perhaps what I saw was a middle ground that more parents can explore. To be fair and honest, I'll report that the mother and child left the cathedral before mass started. I don't know if that was to prevent further disruption or just because the mother had concluded her prayers and was ready to move on. Either way, it was good for her to expose her child to the sights and sounds of church, even if not during a worship service. It was an opportunity for the child to start getting a feel for church—and testing his holy voice.

Pleasant View of the Kingdom

Sometimes the good work that a church does can happen long after the church no longer is a church—at least not in a brick-and-mortar way. That was the case with Pleasant View Baptist Church in Dallas.

For more than twenty years we had seen Pleasant View Baptist as we drove to our own church each week until a move changed our regular route. We were surprised one day when we took the old route and found that the yellow, wood-frame church building was completely gone.

If we had been reading the local newspaper more thoroughly, we would have seen the article reporting that the church, faced with dwindling membership, had voted to disband after 166 years, including some ninety years in that building. What's more, we would have read about the church's wonderful spirit of giving as they used the proceeds from the sale of their property to support ministries both locally and around the world. The pastor's wife said in the article: "I had the joy—because I'm the acting treasurer—of giving money to all the different organizations around the world, helping pastors, helping churches, helping missionaries."

That included an orphanage in Kenya, an international relief fund, an evangelistic organization, and a pregnancy crisis center. Locally, they helped a church that was growing to purchase a new building, while another church got their pews. The pastor of that church said Pleasant View Baptist "is not dead . . . it still lives in us."[2]

The dismantling of Pleasant View presents an interesting challenge—if not a model—for other congregations. If a church can be so gracious and giving in its closing, shouldn't a church that is alive and well be at least as giving and sharing of what it has and who it represents? And what about the people, who we always like to say are "the church" more so than the physical building? It's wonderful to give our possessions and investments to the church when we die, but wouldn't it be nice to do some of that while we are alive—to experience "the joy" of giving, as the pastor's wife described it—and not just within the walls of the church but in the community and the world? And that's important because, as the experience of Pleasant View Baptist shows, walls don't last forever.

Leaning Together

I've enjoyed occasional trips to the Texas Gulf Coast over the years. Some of the natural features that always fascinate me around the central coast town of Rockport are the large groves of live oak trees on the sandy soil up from the beaches. Their trunks are relatively thin, they are short in stature, and their canopies are thick and tangled together as one, creating what could almost serve as a sheltering pavilion.

Most interesting to me is the way they all lean together in the same direction. From inside a passing car, they look as if the wind must be howling. But step out of the car and you find that wind or no wind, the trees are leaning. They're leaning away from the prevailing wind. They've grown up leaning that way, and they've learned to lean together. Alone, they might not stand for long, but in groves, their joined canopies provide mutual support.

I sort of feel that way sometimes in church as we stand together to sing, pray, and read the Scriptures. Individually, our trunks may be thin and breakable, but with our canopies woven together, we can lean away from the buffeting winds of life and toward the living God. We can stand strong together.

The Small and Large of It

"Really big checks, huh?" The bank teller smiled and then laughed a little.

"Yep, and I rushed to get them safely to the bank."

I was happy to play along with her amusement at my two book royalty checks. I get them periodically, and the largest of these two checks was a whopping $1.18—not enough for a small cup of coffee.

No, I didn't really rush them to the bank. The checks came in early May, and I almost lost them until going through a pile of papers—the same pile where I had stashed the letter from the church about the budget and that contained the blue sheet that listed our giving for each of the past seven years. The message was that the church had covered its needs and its ambitions for ministry and mission during the past seven years, and we could do the same over the next seven years if we all just "keep on keeping on," as the saying goes.

LeAnn and I were married in the middle of that seven-year period and our giving records were combined on the blue sheet, so my curiosity prompted me to go to my files and look at my record of personal giving. What I found there between the dollar signs and the decimal points was not only a record of giving but also a recounting of life's ups and downs. Within those seven years I experienced good health and illness, a funeral and a wedding, significant debt and financial solvency.

Lurking behind the numbers was an accounting of my response to those events. There were times when I held back my giving as I faced uncertain events, and times when I gave with reckless abandon. Sometimes I gave with joy, sometimes with grudging hesitation. There were days when I felt like I was giving my last dime, and days when I felt like a king tossing gold upon the altar. But I gave, and I mostly have my parents to thank for that; they helped make it a habitual desire, if not a habitual practice.

I wasn't in the meetings that led to the letter and the blue sheet, but I know the point was not to create pressure or embarrassment. I say that because I've been at the church long enough to know we are not that type of church. Rather, I believe the goal was to stir the imagination of what we can do for the Kingdom—individually and as a community—by recalling what we've already done and what God has done through us.

By giving together as a community, we help fill the gaps for each other as we go through the ebb and flow of life. Just as we can look back and marvel at what the past seven years have brought, none of us knows what the next seven years will bring.

My royalty checks may get bigger, or they may remain small. I could let that embarrass me and get me down, but LeAnn reminds me that even the little checks are a sign that I'm doing what I said I wanted to do, and I'm doing that because I felt it was a calling. She also reminds me that sometimes it is not what our work earns but what our work creates and stirs in others that counts the most.

When I look back at that blue sheet from the church, I'm reminded that if we are following God's calling faithfully, God will faithfully provide. Even when our resources lag and our will falters, God still provides—for us individually and for our community and the Kingdom through us.

A Pentecost Moment

As much as I love our pastor and all of those who preach, pray, and lead us in worship on Sunday mornings, the priests at the Cathedral of Notre Dame in Paris get extra credit for doing all of that while hundreds of tourists mill around looking, talking, and taking pictures.

We were there on a Saturday morning just as the noon mass was starting, and the priest's melodic French voice was ever present through the opening prayers and liturgy of the Word as we walked down the left wall aisle to explore the architecture and history. We stopped for a moment on his right to listen as he spoke in perfect English about the Gospel account of the death of John the Baptist, and then we continued our tour of the tombs and chapels behind the altar.

By the time we came around to the priest's left side, he had come to the Lord's Prayer—the "Our Father," as Catholics call it—and again he spoke in English and said, "This is the prayer that Christ gave to all of us, so please say it with me now in the language of your heart." As he prayed in French, we prayed in English while others around us prayed in German, Spanish, and languages from Asia, Africa, and beyond.

In that moment everyone was speaking in their own tongue, but everyone knew what everyone was saying. It was a Pentecost moment.

Perhaps the takeaway from that visit isn't the priest's amazing concentration but rather his drawing us into the knowledge that God is there for all of us and is with us no matter who we are, where we go, or what we do—whether kneeling in the pews, milling down the aisles, or rushing down the streets outside.

Ambassadors

Sometimes we set out to do something in the name of the Kingdom—and in the church's name, too—and we are reminded that God is way out in front of us.

That was the case when I stopped by the church office after worship to see if there were any guests to visit. Our deacons make what we call "ambassador" visits to guests who have indicated some interest in learning more about the church. It's a low-key effort; we knock on the door, hand them a gift bag with some brochures and a coffee mug, invite them to come back, and we leave. No awkward pressure or pushing.

On this particular Sunday, a guest indicated that he was Baptist and that his wife and children were Catholic. That caught my eye because I first came to our church as a Baptist with a Catholic wife. Our worship style and tendency to follow the liturgical calendar and lectionary of the church at large fit well with our dual allegiances. And the church accepted us as we were; no one tried to turn a Catholic into a Baptist.

Ready to share that story, I knocked on the door of these guests and that's when I discovered that God was already at work. I had expected to speak to the Baptist husband and tell him that our church would be a good fit for him and his Catholic family. Instead, I was met at the door by his Catholic wife and daughter. What's more, she was the one who had brought the family to church, and she did that because she had been a caregiver for one of our members and had learned about the church from that member's family. And when she attended that member's funeral, she was touched by what she experienced and as a result brought her family to church the next day. There was nothing for me to add except to encourage them to come again.

Which brings me back to those ambassador visits, which got their name from 2 Corinthians 5:20: "We are therefore Christ's ambassadors, as though God were making his appeal through us." Ambassadors aren't the big thing; ambassadors are just representatives for the big thing. And ambassadors aren't only deacons on an official visit on a Sunday afternoon. Ambassadors are every one of us, sharing our faith in small subtle ways as we go about our lives—and even as we prepare for the life to come.

Church on the Corner

"So, how's the new year going for you?"

That's as far as I got on the first blog of the new year when I heard a loud crash outside. I stood up to look out the upstairs window and saw two cars wedged together in the middle of the intersection.

"Idiots," I shouted as I bounded down the stairs. "Someone ran the stop sign."

People run the four-way stop at the corner of our property all the time. They usually just scrape the undercarriage of their car on the high ridge of the pavement, but I knew it was just a matter of time before two cars met in the middle.

LeAnn heard the crash, too. We both ran outside to find one of the drivers out of her car inspecting the damage, another still sitting at the steering wheel a little dazed, and drivers of two other cars who had seen the accident and stopped to help. No one was hurt, but neither car was drivable. Phone calls were made, and two policemen arrived for an official inspection.

LeAnn and I found ourselves serving as "hosts" for the event. I escorted one of the drivers to our front porch where she sat in the warm sunshine while she waited for her husband to arrive. LeAnn took a little girl riding in the other car up to the porch swing and read books with her while her mother made calls. When the policemen started pushing some of the plastic and metal debris out of the intersection with their feet, I got a broom and trash can and scooped it all up and carried it away.

As the husband of one of the drivers spoke on the phone with his insurance company, the carillon at the Methodist church nearby chimed the noon hour and then played "God Be With You Till We Meet Again" and "In the Garden." As I listened, I realized that the whole incident had felt and now sounded like "church." It was people helping people in a calm, caring, neighborly manner. And if you recall Christ's commandment to "love your neighbor as yourself," then being "the church" in the neighborhood by just being neighborly is a very real thing.

Which means my initial declaration of "idiots" was neither neighborly nor church-like. It also wasn't true. The two drivers apparently just arrived at the same place at the same time, and neither blamed the other. They both had damage, but they both were okay, and that was all that mattered.

So, back to my initial question about how the new year is going: I'm praying we'll all be more church-like, which is to say, more neighborly, in this year and every year that follows.

Homecoming

Sitting in a pew on the left side of the sanctuary and looking up toward the pulpit, choir loft, and baptistry, the years rolled away and I could see the faces and hear the voices that helped shape my faith and my life.

On several occasions over the previous year I had told LeAnn that I wished I could go back and visit the church I grew up in—to see what had changed but also to remember. Through some connections and persuasion, LeAnn made it happen on a Friday morning as a birthday surprise. This was no simple task, because while the church building is still there, the congregation I grew up in had moved away thirty years earlier. Gaining access was akin to walking up to a house, ringing the doorbell, and saying, "Hi, I used to live here. Mind if I come inside and walk around?" Thankfully, our hosts understood the call of home.

As expected, the tour of the brick-and-mortar buildings triggered memories of flesh-and-blood people. While in the sanctuary I recalled pastors Cloud, Landes, and Fant, who not only preached from the Bible but also taught me to sit still and listen. It was Landes who thrust me under the water one Sunday morning. I thought I was all grown up after that, but a few years later it was pastor Fant's wife who called out my buddy Ken and me for talking too much during the sermon. She had seen it all from her seat in the choir loft.

In the choir room I saw again Bill Green, who got the best out of the youth choir with his boundless energy and charisma. In the children's wing I remembered singing about "sunbeams" and sitting on the floor with a kind old man who helped me make people out of Play-Doh. He always had a toothpick in his pocket with which to carve smiles and wide eyes on blank faces.

In the chapel I remembered Wednesday evening prayer meetings and summer mornings where we congregated for Scriptures and songs at the start of Vacation Bible School. And I remembered the sorrow of sitting there on an Easter weekend to say goodbye to my little sister who was taken from this life too soon.

Outside the chapel we stopped at the stairs leading down to The Fisherman's Net youth center in the basement. Our guide said they don't use it much and there wouldn't be anything to see, but looking down the stairs I could almost hear bouncing ping-pong balls and movies threading through projectors and the guitar of Billy Crockett on a Friday night. And in the middle of it all was youth minister Kenny Wood, who taught us that church had room for both reverence and laughter.

We didn't roam the upstairs hallways, but I knew that up there were the Sunday school rooms where I experienced much more than I learned: where I received a silver dollar for memorizing all the books of the Bible in order; where teacher Bob Dietz gave me strength in the weeks after my sister died; where Ken and I learned in a tough "for credit" class that we were not destined to be Bible scholars.

The tour not only brought back these memories but also reinforced for me the importance of these places and people we call church. They're not just Sunday-only places where we go to sing, listen, and receive "a dose of the ghost" to get us through another week. They're not daycares for children and social clubs for adults. They're lifelong schools where we keep coming to learn, grow, question, discern, stretch, test, try, and fail at being who God created us to be.

Five Bucks for Jesus

On a Wednesday night I stepped out of the garage to roll the big green trash can out to the curb, and from the darkness I heard a voice: "Excuse me, sir."

I looked up and saw a man walking down the middle of the street and then turning onto our driveway.

"I was wondering if you could help me? I've run out of gas, and I need to go to Greenville." (That's a town forty miles from where we live.)

We live on the edge of downtown Garland, with a convenience store and gas station nearby. It's not unusual to see someone walking by, but it's startling at night when someone suddenly appears and calls out to you. My initial nervousness was relieved a little by his next words: "You remember me—I offered to help you clean out your flowerbeds one day." I thought about it and did remember a few offers like that, none that I've ever taken, so he might have been telling the truth.

I asked him if he had something to carry the gas in, and when he said he did, I told him to wait a moment and I went back in the house. As I was getting my wallet, LeAnn asked what was up.

"There's a man walking by who needs money for gas. It may be a scam, or he may be Jesus. I'm going to give him five dollars."

Back outside, I handed him the five, and when he looked at it in the dim light, he wasn't happy.

"I need more than that to get to Greenville. Don't you have more?"

"No sir, that's all I have."

That was a lie. I did have more. I had enough to buy him a tank of gas. I had enough to call him a cab. I had enough to buy him a new car . . . to charter a private plane or helicopter and land him wherever he wanted to go. I could have done any of that, but I wasn't going to give him more than five dollars. I figured that if he was being honest and if his vehicle got twenty miles per gallon, five dollars would get him to Greenville. And if he was being dishonest, then five dollars would not get him in too much trouble.

There was another option: If he was serious about going to Greenville, I could have given him a ride. Sometimes we're bold and make such an offer because we really do want to help. But other times we make the offer to call a bluff. Someone asks for money for food, we offer to take them to get something to eat, and when they decline, we think, "Busted." But I didn't make that offer on this night because I really didn't want to go to Greenville. I really didn't want to help. I just wanted to be left alone.

His irritation at my measly five dollars irritated me right back, and for a split second I wanted to take it out of his hand and go back inside. A man once asked me for money on a downtown Dallas street on a freezing night after work. He didn't have a warm coat or gloves, and I handed him my gloves. He took them but didn't put them on, and when he still wanted money and I rejected him, he got angry. I got angry too, and I grabbed my gloves back and walked away.

On this night I let the man keep the five dollars and said, "Good luck." He walked away still angry or at least disappointed. I'm thinking Jesus was disappointed too—not in the size of my offering but in the smallness of my heart.

The Real Work Begins

For a few years at Christmas our church has hosted an interactive Bethlehem experience called "One Starry Night." One of the small miracles that occurs each time is that after a year of planning and preparation, a full week of setting up, and three hours with hundreds of people in the marketplace, it takes just ninety minutes to put it all away.

As soon as our King Herod declares, "Bethlehem is now under curfew," and the last guest has cleared the market, the lights come on and every one scrambles to take down the tents, pack up the crafts and supplies, and cart everything away. We even have a few volunteers who come specifically to help "sack the village," as I describe it.

I've made this speedy takedown a special mission of mine—for reasons that I will explain in a moment—but I have to admit that I anticipate putting Christmas away as much if not more than bringing it all out. While I do love Christmas and all its sights and sounds and especially the tastes and smells, I always look forward to the ordinary flow of life that returns after the holidays. I don't think that makes me a Grinch, and I hope it doesn't make me a Scrooge, but during Christmas it seems that so much grinds to a halt while there is still important work that needs to be done.

I'm usually ready to sing "Joy to the World" in a different way when the calendar changes, but one year on New Year's Day as we began packing away Christmas at home, I remembered the words of Howard Thurman's poem, "The Work of Christmas":

When the song of the angels is stilled,
When the star in the sky is gone,
When the kings and princes are home,
When the shepherds are back with their flock,
The work of Christmas begins:
To find the lost,
To heal the broken,
To feed the hungry,
To release the prisoner,
To rebuild the nations,
To bring peace among people,
To make music in the heart.[3]

The first year we did One Starry Night, we cleaned it up quickly because every-thing had to be back to normal for church on Sunday morning. But the next year we worked even faster because Gateway of Grace, a ministry that works with refugees, was set to host a Christmas luncheon the next day for some three hundred people from ten countries. After we had removed all traces of Bethlehem, some of us stayed a while longer to help roll out tables and chairs. We did it because Gateway of Grace is truly doing the work of Christmas as it helps refugees from around the world find a safe footing in North Texas.

That same year the ongoing work of Christmas was magnified by tornadoes that struck North Texas the night after Christmas, leaving hundreds of families who had just opened new gifts with nothing but new sorrows. Just two blocks from our house, our city park was the resource center for people who needed food, clothing, and shelter, and untold numbers of people from the community and beyond answered the call to do the work of Christmas in providing resources.

LeAnn and I experienced the work of Christmas in other new ways that same year. On New Year's Eve our neighbors across the street invited us to a celebration with their extended family. Their language and food are different from ours, but we understood their laughter and hospitality and together experienced that last item in Thurman's poem: "music in the heart."

On New Year's Day a longtime friend stopped by with cornbread and a pot of black-eyed peas, and we spent the noontime sharing stories of life's love and loss. And the next morning we found ourselves at a "Prayer on the Square" gathering in a downtown restaurant, where Tammy, our gracious host, kept coffee cups full while a couple of dozen concerned citizens prayed for their community—good Christmas work for sure.

So, while most of us pack Christmas away for another year, let's not pack away the work of Christmas. There is plenty more to do on that list in Thurman's poem.

Love Is the Common Ground

On one summer's road trip we made a side jaunt to visit an old friend. He had left Dallas some years ago after a lifetime of city living and we found him enjoying himself in a smaller, quieter place. During the hour we spent with him, he told us about his new life in the town and the pleasure he is getting from becoming a part of a small community that has benefitted from his experience, perspective, and energy. But what he was most interested in talking about was his church.

He is a Baptist like us, and when he got to his new hometown he looked around and found there was only one Baptist church. So, he went to visit and quickly discovered that it was, well, different from what he was accustomed to. Their worship style was different, and on some theological points he did not see the world as they did. In fact, his status as a single male has since prevented him from serving in some ways.

If faced with that obstacle, some of us might decide to worship elsewhere—to travel a distance to attend another Baptist church or check out another denomination that aligns with our style and beliefs. But he stayed and stuck with them because he discovered that this church has a huge heart for the community and the world, and that is a place of common ground. And so he has become an active member of the church and a leader in many of its mission efforts both in the community and abroad.

It's a wonderful example for anyone who has found themselves at odds with their church, their neighbors, their family. It's tempting, and perhaps human nature, to focus on our differences and let them be what defines our relationship—and thus what keeps us apart. In fact, it's often easier to turn and leave than it is to set aside the differences and embrace all that is still so good.

Our friend has taught us that the common ground of Christian love is more stable than the shifting sands of theology and tradition. That doesn't mean that we won't still stumble over those differences; they are still there. Our friend misses the church traditions he had grown to love, but he's grown to love the work and the community he has found in his new church. And no one has pushed him to change his beliefs, because respect and tolerance are also part of that common ground they share.

Jump-Start

"What is the best visitor gift you've received when visiting a new church?"

That was the question a director of a college and young adult ministry at a church in a college town posed on social media, and she received a variety of answers from her far-flung friends across the country:

- "Jar of homemade jam."
- "Homemade ramen from a church in Japan. Oh, and Japanese candy."
- "Coffee mug hand-delivered to my house the next day by a member who gave me her phone number. So awesome!"

A couple of people answered by telling what their church does or what they have done personally: "We give out homemade bread at our church. It's great." And, "I remember noticing how well a visitor sang and told them about the choir and Sunday School and UMW. They became members for years. I think feeling truly welcomed is the best."

My own answer came instantly, and it was surprising because it came from a memory I hadn't recalled in decades: "A jump-start for my car."

It was Waco, Texas, circa 1983, and I pulled into a church parking lot for a Sunday evening service but forgot to turn off my car lights. This was back when car lights didn't turn off automatically, and it wasn't unusual at events and even at church for someone to step up to the microphone and announce, "If you drive a brown Chevy Malibu, license number TYY-999, you've left your lights on." And the crowd would hush for a moment as everyone thought, "Is that mine?" And then relieved, they'd look around with pity to see who had been so absentminded.

But on this night, there was no announcement and the service went on as planned without interruption. When I got out to the parking lot afterward, I was met at the side of my brown Chevy Malibu by a man with his own hood up and jumper cables in hand. He explained that they don't interrupt the service; they meet people at their car and jump-start them if needed, and indeed it was needed. He hooked me up and got me started. As I thanked him, he said, "You might want to let it run awhile to make sure you're fully charged. And do come back to see us."

Looking back at all the answers to the question, it seems like they all fall under the heading of "jump-start." Isn't a friendly gesture from a stranger—a loaf of bread, a jar of jam, a compliment, an invitation—a jump-start to our spirit? Don't those offerings of hospitality make us feel like we matter, that we're appreciated, and that we belong? Don't we all long for community, even if we still want to choose how much and when?

Isn't offering a jump-start generally what churches should be about? Providing the tools for a closer walk with Christ, a place of fellowship and sharing with others, a safe place to pop up the hood on our weak, beaten spirits and get a recharge through the love of each other and the love of Christ?

And how about routine maintenance? A jump-start is only, well, a start. There's so much more on the service menu:

• A time of quiet in a noisy world
• A place of safety in a dangerous age
• A ray of hope when all seems hopeless
• An embrace of unconditional love when we feel unlovable
• A forum for discernment when searching for answers to hard questions
• An outlet for sharing the love of Christ in the community

I did take the advice of the kind man in the parking lot of the Waco church. I drove around awhile until I was certain my battery was recharged, and I did visit again. I didn't join that church because I was moving to Dallas in a few months, but I searched for and found a church that not only jump-starts me when needed but keeps me fueled and going.

True Colors

One late winter day while getting ready to go to an NCAA basketball tournament, I had to make a fashion decision: Wear an official green or gold T-shirt from my alma mater, wear a regular green shirt but unmarked, or just wear one of my usual shirts, most of which are some shade of blue. I chose to wear an unmarked green shirt because it was comfortable and warm. And I reasoned that with much of the crowd wearing burnt orange, people would know by my plain green shirt who I represent.

Years ago I wrote a memoir for the founder of a large Dallas business and was intrigued that he did not want his company to be known as "a Christian business." He was a devout man and had surrounded himself with colleagues of similar character and beliefs, but when some people in the business wanted to make an official statement of Christian values, he said no. There were practical reasons: He didn't want to be labeled a hypocrite if someone made a mistake, or if the company had to make an honest but tough decision. He also didn't want to use Christ as a marketing ploy as some businesses do. But more than anything else, he just wanted his company's actions to speak for themselves rather than some official banner.

A friend who spent years doing mission work among Muslims in Indonesia said he learned to describe himself as a "Christ follower" and not a Christian. The Muslims understand who Christ is, and they respect him as a great prophet. But Christians? Well, they hear us say that America is a "Christian nation," and then they see our television shows and movies laden with violence, greed, and immorality, and they draw understandably negative conclusions.

Which all goes to say that having official colors, logos, and mottos doesn't say as much as how you live and how you treat people—whether doing business with them, ministering to them, or just being their neighbor. In fact, you can learn more about someone—who they are, what they need, how you can be better neighbors— by listening to them than you can by telling them who you are or waving your flag in their face.

A Jesus House

One Sunday morning as we were getting ready for church, the doorbell rang and LeAnn opened the door to find Ms. Ortiz, our neighbor across the street, with a foil-wrapped package of homemade tamales. As she handed them to LeAnn, she said, "This is a Jesus house, right?"

"Yes," was the answer. After all, we were getting ready for church. But truly, we do want ours to be a "Jesus house," and with God's help and grace it is.

We don't know Ms. Ortiz very well. Our conversations have been limited due to a language difference, so we mostly just wave from across the street. Shortly after moving into the neighborhood, we tried to help her catch her runaway dog. We failed, but she thanked us with a hug and an "I love you." On many Saturday evenings, members of her church arrive at her house with Bibles and casserole dishes. When the weather is cool, we hear songs of praise in Spanish coming through the open doors and windows. I suspect that if we were to go over there during one of those worship gatherings we'd be welcomed enthusiastically, even though our language and worship style are different. I say that because I believe hers is a "Jesus house" too.

So, what does a "Jesus house" look like? I believe it is welcoming—as welcoming as Jesus was to everyone he met regardless of their background, transgressions, afflictions, or shortcomings.

It was in that spirit that our church changed our bylaws some years back to extend church membership to those who have been baptized in other Christian traditions, who do not wish to be re-baptized by immersion, but who affirm their profession of faith in Christ as their Lord and Savior. We didn't change the way we have always baptized those who come to a faith in Christ through the doors of our church: believer's baptism by immersion. We just acknowledged the experience of those who have come to faith in other ways.

We hold tightly to the immersion tradition because it is the Baptist way, but it's not necessarily Jesus' way. The Gospels tell us that Jesus was baptized by John in the River Jordan, but nowhere does Jesus say that we must be baptized in precisely the same manner. Even John downgraded the role of baptism when he said to his followers, "I baptize you with water, but he will baptize you with the Holy Spirit" (Mark 1:8).

And while baptism was one of the instructions that Jesus left with his disciples—"Therefore go and make disciples of all nations, baptizing them in the name of the Father and of the Son and of the Holy Spirit, and teaching them to obey everything I have commanded you" (Matt. 28:19)—there are no specific instructions for how and when baptism should occur.

So what *did* Jesus command? When asked about the greatest commandments in the Law, he was very clear: "'Love the Lord your God with all your heart and with all your soul and with all your mind.' This is the first and greatest commandment. And the second is like it: 'Love your neighbor as yourself'" (Matt. 22:37–39).

That is what a Jesus house looks like.

There's Not Just One Way

One year during March Madness, a lot of college basketball teams were wearing T-shirts that said "The _____ Way," such as "The Wolverine Way," "The Badger Way," "The Cardinal Way." The only difference was the color of the shirt and the name of the mascot. Otherwise, the design was identical.

I first saw the T-shirts worn by our Baylor team toward the end of the Big 12 tournament. I thought they had something unique and special with "The Bears Way" shirts until I watched the NCAA Tournament Selection Show and saw that schools from coast to coast had the same style shirts.

Apparently, Adidas provided the shirts to teams that buy their equipment. I have just two things to say about that: Shame on the teams for being so easily bamboozled into a one-style-suits-all spirit gimmick, and shame on Adidas for trying to make everyone look the same. Every school has its own unique cultures and traditions, and every school should express that in its own way.

I feel the same way when someone in the media or theological circles or even from a local church tries to paint all the members of a religion or a denomination with the same brush. The truth is that regardless of the affiliation, no two Baptist or Catholic or Presbyterian or (fill in the blank) churches are exactly alike. Each has its own personality and culture and way of expressing "the way," as led by group experience and the Holy Spirit.

While our ways may be different, the love, caring, and hospitality that we model come from the same divine source. Clearly, while we all may wear the same label of Christian and be clothed in the same Holy Spirit, ours is not a one-size-fits-all or a one-style-suits-all faith. Don't let Adidas or anyone else tell you different.

Long Shots and Long Views

The funeral of a family member had us attending a luncheon at the church where my grandparents were members. It had been years since I'd been in the church, including the family life center where the luncheon was held. I found that interesting because it is a building I remember my grandfather grumbling about more than thirty years earlier during the capital campaign to fund its construction.

Talking to the pastor of the church over lunch, I shared that bit of family history, and he said the facility was recently renovated because it had been well used by the church and the community over the years. Most notably, the gym hosts an Upward Basketball league that on many Saturdays draws 1,500 adults and children from around the city. In other words, the family life center is the focal point of a vibrant community ministry.

I'm not advocating for family life centers and sports leagues at my church or any other church. But what seems to have been true three decades ago is true today: Community ministry comes in many different forms, and sometimes it requires thinking outside the box and looking well beyond the horizon.

At our church we've hosted patriotic concerts and barbecue dinners on July 4th, food trucks on Sundays after worship, monthly jazz concerts, mission tradeshows, and interactive Bethlehem villages at Christmas. These and other events have become popular draws for the surrounding neighborhood and the community-at-large. As with the family life center I visited, not everyone may see the potential of these events right away and thus the need for the time, energy, and money we put into them. On the other hand, lots of folks have volunteered to help with these events. They understand the value of reaching the community—and sharing the message and love of Christ—through an event that is at the church but doesn't look and feel like church.

I was too young to care about my grandfather's objections to the family life center, but I'm sure it came out of his Depression-era frugality and his leaning toward more traditional ministries of the day such as revival meetings. For all I know, he trusted the leadership and new ideas of younger people in the church and supported the building campaign in the end. I know for a fact that he was a big basketball fan, and if he were here today, he'd probably love the idea of young people from around the community shooting hoops at his church.

Front and Center

On a bright, sunny Sunday, everyone in the church gathered in the sanctuary for a picture of the entire congregation. We had one service that day so that everyone would be there. The result is a beautiful, lively photo showing the church as it truly is—the people and not the building. Still, I cringe when I see it because standing front and center are LeAnn and me.

On photo day we should have been in our regular places: me in the balcony and LeAnn with the choir. But we volunteered to help bring in the preschoolers, and that put us up front. I had lobbied that we release the kids to their families and melt into the congregation ourselves, but people who know better about children said we should stay with them. So, there we are, front and center.

It was an unintended fluke, and anyone who knows me well knows the last place I ever want to be in any photo or any room or any event is front and center. I don't do selfies. I don't jump to the front and volunteer to be the leader. My mother can tell you that when I was in the children's choir at our church growing up, I stood at the end of the row, and not just the end but behind the person at the end of the row. I'm happy to be standing on the fringes or even out of sight.

My fear is that decades from now someone will study the photo and ask, "So, this man standing in front in the dark suit and the gray hair . . . he obviously is the pastor, but I don't remember him at all. When was he the pastor?" If they looked closely to the right and left, they'd find the real pastor and associate pastor and minister of music standing in the aisles with the people of the church.

In the early twentieth century when churches took grainy black-and-white photographs of their congregations for posterity, the protocol of the day usually had the pastor and his wife positioned front and center. That's fine with me because pastors easily earn that privilege. Standing front and center, they rightfully can say, "These are all the people with their messy lives that I have to tend to on a daily basis."

But it says something about our church that everyone gets to stand front and center from time to time. We have deacons, committee members, and volunteers who work shoulder to shoulder with the paid ministers and staff to keep the church and its mission moving forward. On any given day, any one person among those hundreds of people is working front and center on something, even if no one knows it.

So, this message needs to go into a time capsule with that photo: No, that is not the pastor standing in the front of the church in the photograph taken in 2018. Those are just people who were trying to help out and landed in the wrong place at the wrong time. But happily, they were in a good church at a good time.

Checking Boxes

Have you checked your passport recently? I don't travel internationally very often and assumed I was good to go for a trip to Canada one fall. But when I pulled my passport out of the bottom of my desk drawer, I discovered it had expired. So, I had to hustle to get it renewed.

Other than the deadline, the renewal application was actually easy because nothing important had changed: name, birthdate, height, address, Social Security number. The application didn't ask about weight: it hadn't changed either, but I'm not bragging because that is mostly genetics. But I was asked about my hair color, which made me pause. For the first time in my life I had to skip the "brown" box and check "gray." My hair began changing color twenty-five years ago, starting in the front and working toward the back, following the same pattern and timing as my father.

The passport application asked about eye color: my eyes are different shades of blue, depending on what I'm wearing. It didn't mention teeth, but if it did, I'd have to claim some replacements. It's weird to think about yourself as a car that no longer has all of its factory-installed parts.

The application didn't inquire about faith or denomination. This checkbox used to be included on lots of applications and perhaps even for passports, but no more. And that's good because there are too many stereotypes rolled into that, and stereotypes often are based on ugly extremes. I could check a box for "Baptist" and a customs agent might put me on a watch list for gun-toting, homophobic, xeno-phobic, male chauvinistic racists because that's how we're often painted based on some of the more vocally outrageous among our numbers.

But I'm also glad the passport application didn't ask about religious affiliation, because the Baptist I am today is not the Baptist I was when I was ten or twenty or even forty or fifty. And most of that is because I've more fully embraced what I believe to be the true meaning of being a Baptist, which is to tend to my own faith and let my neighbors tend to theirs. But then that sounds like Baptists have nothing to do but pat ourselves on the back and sing "hallelujah" because we're saved; we've cleared customs, and our passports are good for all eternity. But that's not what I'm saying.

My personal faith—which also is very much hereditary and like my hair color is changing through the daily experiences of life—tells me that while I shouldn't care about the boxes that others check on their passports, I definitely should care about the boxes we force others into by our words, our silence, our actions, and our inaction. Those boxes include poverty and all that encompasses, along with injustice and marginalization. These are not problems we can solve by just praying from our cloisters or by going door to door and changing boxes from "None" to "Baptist." These are problems that require our hands and feet in the acts of delivering shelter, food, education, medicine, opportunity, hope, respect, and love. Those last four items on the list are perhaps the most powerful and yet require the least resources. You'd think they'd be easy, but they require that we denounce and disprove those stereotypes that plague us.

When I got my first passport in the 1980s, I believed my faith was defined mostly by my personal relationship with God through Jesus Christ. That relationship is still paramount, but today I believe it is defined by my relationship with my neighbors. It's a faith turned inside out—a faith lived outside the checked boxes.

And Now Let Us Pray . . .

I don't recall exactly when it started, but sometime early in our relationship LeAnn and I began holding hands whenever there was a prayer being spoken. Certainly it was a sign of our shared faith, but I confess that early on it was a good excuse to lace our fingers together as couples do when they're beginning to feel connected. We were sort of hiding out in the beginning, and prayer time offered a chance to make contact while "every head was bowed and every eye was closed," as evangelists used to say.

We hold hands in prayer all the time now whether saying grace at home, standing in prayer at church, sitting in Sunday school, or attending a civic meeting or athletic event that still includes an invocation. Sometimes if we're in the same room but not side by side, we'll scoot toward each other and slip our hands together just before the prayer. Somehow it completes the prayer for us—as if maybe two are stronger than one.

It has become such a regular thing that sometimes when we are not together, I have to push back against the impulse to grab a hand. Of course, there are times when we do reach across the aisles and around the tables to grasp hands and pray with people who aren't our spouses or who we don't even know. A former pastor was fond of having everyone join hands across the sanctuary to sing "Blest Be the Tie That Binds." That's mostly a prayer set to music, and we could feel the Spirit shared in the physical connections.

I got the same feeling at the end of Scout troop meetings when we would stand in a circle, cross arms, grasp hands, and recite the Scoutmaster's Benediction: "And now, may the great Master of all scouts be with us until we meet again." It was a way of uniting as a community and speaking to God in one strong voice made from many.

My years living near the Catholic faith introduced me to communal, liturgical prayers. We evangelicals often dismiss them as "rote," but I grew to find peace and comfort in the familiar words and rhythms spoken in unison. It was like speaking to the God who is eternal and constant with words that were eternal and constant. The irony was that my Catholic mother-in-law at the time would sometimes ask me to say grace at the table. She said she liked my "beautiful" prayers, which I think meant my freestyle evangelical delivery was a nice change from the standard table blessing.

Even so, my freestyle prayers were built from what I heard growing up. I was raised in a family that prayed, and that meant there were familiar patterns and phrases. On my father's side, Grandpa would always ask God to "lead, guide, and direct us," which if you think about it pretty much covers all the bases of God's sovereignty. And on my mother's side, Grandad couldn't bless the roast beef and vegetables without tearing up. I never asked him about that, but my guess is he prayed with a heart full of gratitude—not a bad way to go about it.

My prayer life today is a mixture of these and other influences, the most recent addition being this habit of holding hands. So, you better watch out if you're standing next to me during a prayer.

Passing the Peace

The doorbell rang on the Saturday afternoon before Easter and I looked down from the upstairs window to see two nicely but simply dressed women, one with a satchel and the other with a small stack of papers in her hand. Apparently, they rang the doorbell and then stepped back off the porch to wait.

"I'll get it," I shouted and walked quickly down the stairs to the front door. LeAnn was working in the kitchen, and I didn't want her to stop what she was doing. But more than that, I knew from looking out the window what was waiting and what to do about it.

And I was right: It was two women going door to door on behalf of Jesus and God. On past visits they had made a brief statement of faith and offered some literature, but this time they handed me a small folded flyer and pointed to a specific time and date for a talk titled, "How to Cultivate Peace in an Angry World."

"That's a timely topic," I said in total honesty, to which one of the women said, "We think it will be of great interest and help to a lot of people. There's so much anger, fear, and uncertainty in the world."

I looked at the time and date again, and it was the next morning—Easter Sunday. I said, "Oh, this is tomorrow. We'll be at our church tomorrow." That was a kinder way of saying, "We've got this faith thing covered and we're not the heathen you might think we are, and so, no, we won't be coming to the talk tomorrow." And then I thanked them for stopping and wished them a blessed Easter. I admire what they do, and I usually tell them so, but I forgot to do that this time.

The Monday after Easter I saw the flyer in the stack of stuff on the kitchen counter and looked at it again. I looked up their denomination on the internet and found that "How to Cultivate Peace in an Angry World" was their worldwide focus on Easter weekend.

Thinking about that and our own Easter observance, I realize we are really working toward the same goal and we have Christ as the example to follow. Didn't Jesus' ministry focus on cultivating peace? Wasn't the world he came into angry—as well as fearful, hateful, hungry, hurting? Wasn't his death on the cross the culmination of that anger, and his resurrection the ultimate gift of peace? Didn't he return and greet his disciples with the words, "Peace be with you"?

There are many ways to learn about and practice passing the peace: Bible studies and sermons, worship and seminars, music and prayers. They all resonate in different ways with different people, and they're all good. But then comes the actual passing of peace, and that requires getting up and getting out. We pass the peace in church, but we're mostly "preaching to the choir"—as the old saying goes. We pass the peace in our neighborhoods, workplaces, and communities just by treating those we come into contact with as Christ would—with compassion, respect, and trust.

But to cultivate peace in an angry world, you have to bravely go out into that angry world. That takes faith and courage and not being afraid of who or what is waiting on the other side of a closed door. Those two women had it easy with me, but I can't imagine what they face sometimes. I pray for their peace and safety as they go.

Mountains and Valleys

While lying on a cot on a Sunday morning during one of our church's periodic blood drives, I looked up and found that I was resting between two of the large paintings that grace this room used for receptions and special events. One painting depicts a sunny garden wedding celebration and the other a gray deathbed scene. As I looked at the two paintings, the portable stereo brought by the technicians from the blood bank was playing "Ain't No Mountain High Enough."

The song is a love anthem from 1970 with Diana Ross belting out the chorus with its less-than-poetic grammar about how no mountains, valleys, or rivers can keep lovers apart. Pop lyrics for sure, and if there hadn't been a tube hanging out of my arm, I might have raised my hands and swayed. But as I listened to the song about mountains and valleys, while viewing those scenes of joy and sorrow, I was reminded of Paul's more poetic words from the book of Romans: "For I am convinced that neither death nor life, neither angels nor demons, neither the present nor the future, nor any powers, neither height nor depth, nor anything else in all creation, will be able to separate us from the love of God that is in Christ Jesus our Lord" (Rom. 8:38-39).

I've lived in both those painted scenes. I've hung my head in the sorrowful valley, and I've stood on the mountaintop hand-in-hand with new love. It's been valleys and mountains, demons and angels, death and life. But the truth is that most of us spend our days on the slopes and terraces between the mountains and valleys, the celebrations and sorrows. Most of the time we're on our way up or on our way down.

Or, we're resting on a ledge trying to map out the next part of the journey with the mountaintop our preferred destination. These places of rest and preparation are also depicted in the paintings in that room: a family dedication, a baptism. But the largest painting encompasses both pop song lyrics and Paul's letter of hope. It's a scene of a Communion table with people of all ages gathered before the bread and the cup representing God's gift through Christ's sacrifice.

That scene is God's love song to us—God's assurance that nothing can separate us from God's love. It is our resting place between the mountains and valleys, the angels and demons. It is where we stand, if we're willing, every day of our life.

Breaking Rules

I can't imagine what it's like inside Garrett's head—the way he sees the world. But I know something of how the world sounds to him because he turns what he experiences into amazing music. We got a good dose of this at his master's jazz composition recital, where he conducted three original pieces he had composed and three he had arranged. I won't try to explain what we heard, because music is meant to be experienced and not explained in words.

Something I can describe, however, is the way Garrett broke the rules—doing things with the saxophone that I was taught not to do and I'm sure he was taught not to do. From the beginning of the recital with Garrett's first solo and later with some of his other soloists, there were sounds made—I think—by biting the mouthpiece, squeezing the reed, overblowing the horn, and using finger combinations that are usually mistakes. The result was squeals, squawks, and groans that junior high band directors and private lesson teachers work hard to make sure young instrumentalists never make; sounds that have no place in a Sousa march or a Holst suite. And yet when written into a jazz chart by Garrett they become cries for freedom and acceptance, moans of sorrow, shouts of anger, squeals of rapture. They become music.

I can play the sax but I'm no musician, so I turned to writing. There, too, I was given rules to follow. I was taught to build tidy little noun-verb-noun sentences, and then compound them and adorn them with prepositions and colorful adjectives. I followed the rules and made good grades on compositions and term papers. But then I started reading classic novels and new works and—wait a minute, these writers are not following the rules. This one is writing rambling, run-on sentences that go on and on and before long I've forgotten what the subject of the sentence is, but my head is tingling with an understanding of what the writer is feeling and trying to make me feel. Or this writer? Fragments. Just small pieces. Incomplete thoughts . . . Not the way I was taught, and yet it is literature.

I grew up in the church and was taught as a child in a simple way about how Jesus loved everyone. But then I got older and started digging deeper and discovered that when our teachers said, "Jesus loved the people," they meant he loved those other people too—the ones who we've grown up to distrust, disdain, or disregard because they're different; the ones who society and well-meaning people tell us don't live right, don't believe what we believe, and are dangerous to be around. They need our help to become good people just like us, and then they'll be ready for our friendship and love.

Maybe I've grown tired or lazy, but I don't want to play by those rules any longer. I'm tired of saying "yes" to this person and "no" to that one. I'm tired of trying to play God and separating the sheep from the goats. Jesus didn't play God, not the way the Jews of his day expected. He broke the rules they had known and observed for centuries because those rules distracted people from the two that mattered most: love God and love each other the way you wish to be loved.

It's simple and straightforward, and yet it's hard. We like rules because they keep us safe and safely in our comfort zone. Breaking the rules goes against our habits and even our human nature. It rubs us the wrong way—like discordant sounds from a saxophone or over-long sentences in a book. But if we listen and read with our hearts and not just our heads, we might just hear the music and read the poetry that is in the lives of those around us, the ones whom Jesus told us to love.

Garrett broke the rules, and listening to his music challenged, moved, entertained, pushed to the ground, and lifted to the heavens—sort of like what happens when you live the gospel.

Don't Miss Out

We lost a decade. We weren't angry, bitter, or upset. We were just busy with life, and a day became a week and then a month and then a year, until ten years had passed.

I'm talking about my best friend, Ken, and myself. Somewhere along the way we both got embarrassed and didn't know how to reconnect until one glorious day when one of us finally said "enough" and sent an email. It doesn't matter which one of us, because as it turns out, we both had a finger on the send button. We both knew we were missing out.

It was just in the nick of time because right as we reconnected, Ken lost a close friend and colleague. Not long after that, I had my own loss. Life was twisting and turning, and we both needed someone to help keep us steady and balanced—or to be with us if we wanted to rant and cry. We quickly discovered, too, that we both needed someone to laugh with. Our friendship began in the seventh grade and was built on laughter—we'd forgotten how much we enjoyed that. In time, I needed someone to encourage me as I moved toward a new love and life, and when the big day came, I needed Ken to stand with me as a witness to God's love and grace.

Is there someone you are missing? Someone who you've let slip out of your life? A family member, a good old friend?

Maybe someone at church because, yes, drifting apart does happen at church. We become busy with committees and fellowships and places of ministry and responsibility, and we look up and discover that someone hasn't been around for a while. We assume they're okay or that someone else is keeping up with them, so we keep pushing ahead because, after all, we're doing the work of the church, right? Except that keeping up with each other *is* the work of the church.

If the church is to be the body of Christ on earth, then we need all of our members—both literal and figurative. We may be the one who has slipped away, and if so, we may not realize how much we are missing and how much we are missed. The fact is that the body of Christ is never complete so long as someone—anyone—goes missing.

So what does being the body of Christ have to do with Ken and me? Did I mention that we never lived in the same neighborhood, and until we were roommates in college, we never attended the same school? And even then, we took just two classes together. Our common ground was the church where we grew up. While we don't attend the same church now, we are still bonded by our faith and our friendship.

Don't make the mistake we made. Don't lose the blessings of being the body of Christ because you are busy or distracted or embarrassed. Make a call, send an email, knock on a door. Reclaim a family member, a best friend.

Random Beauty

Sitting in the chapel on a Sunday afternoon before an ordination service, I found myself continuing a study I began during a previous visit there: looking for a pattern in the small square panes of stained glass in the windows. It's an odd habit of mine, along with counting things.

The first task was to determine how many colors there are. There are six: soft shades of pink, orange, green, white, blue, and yellow. Next, I looked at a green pane in one window and a green pane in another to see if the colors touching them match. They don't. I did this several times on several windows and found there is no pattern at all. The six colors are set into the lead frames in a beautifully random fashion.

I saw the same random beauty as I watched the line of well-wishers quietly moving down the aisle to lay hands on the young minister being ordained: people of different ages, sizes, colors, backgrounds, interests. Ours is not a cookie-cutter faith, so it makes sense that we're not a cookie-cutter church. We fit together, not because we look or sound alike, but because we complement each other. Side by side, we bring out the best qualities in each other like the panes of glass in the chapel windows.

The older I get, the more I appreciate these differences. When we're younger we tend to seek out those who look and act like us, or who we want to look and act like. We're Dr. Seuss' "Sneetches," wanting a star on our belly that looks just like the stars on all the other bellies. But beauty is more than skin deep, and our ideas are beautifully different as well. This comes to light every Sunday in our Bible study class when we share our diverse views on whatever Scripture we're studying. I never leave feeling alienated or disillusioned. Rather, I'm provoked and challenged.

I believe that's exactly where God wants us to be: thinking, pondering, and questioning—not passive, submissive, or ambivalent. Just as a car steers more easily the faster the wheels are turning, it's easier to steer our hearts toward the truth when our minds are engaged and active. It also takes friction to gain traction, and sometimes the best friction comes from those who rub us in a different way—even the wrong way.

Consider the one little pane of glass in a window on the north wall of the chapel that is a much deeper shade than any of the others. I don't know if it is a replacement pane or one that was set in the window from the start, but it catches my attention every time I'm there. In fact, it was that unique pane of glass that first provoked me to look for patterns and discover the random beauty in these stained-glass creations.

Dancing Through Life

On a Monday night we turned on the television to watch our usual program and caught the last minute of *Dancing with the Stars*. If I heard right, one of the female contestants said, and I'm paraphrasing, "This program has nothing at all to do with dancing. It's all about the relationships and bonds we form."

Really? That sounded like a stretch to me because it does seem to be a competition where you get booted if you don't dance well. But the more I've thought about it, the more that statement has intrigued me. I've started to wonder what would happen if we applied that philosophy to everything we do. What if when we go to work, when we go shopping, when we go to the football game, when we work in the yard, when we do whatever we do . . . it's not really about the product we make or the things we buy or the game we win or the tasks we complete, but instead it's about the contacts we make and the relationships we create?

Earlier that same Monday, LeAnn and I had been to the State Fair of Texas, and while we had a great time, two things stand out when viewing the day through the prism of "relationship." First, we rode the train from our suburb to the fair. When we stopped at a station near downtown Dallas, our friend Paul hopped aboard. We had an unexpected and enjoyable conversation until we parted ways downtown. Paul sent an email later telling us how much he enjoyed the visit.

Late in the afternoon at the fair, a man in an apron asked if we could help him with bus fare to get home. I gave him some loose change, and then as he walked away, I grumbled that perhaps he found the apron and his real "job" at the fair was shaking people down. But our paths crossed once more and he said, "Thank you again for your help." We stopped and talked for a moment, found out he works in food service at the fair, and we let go of the dollar coins we forgot were in our pockets. He thanked us again and said, "God bless you."

Jesus demonstrates the relational mindset throughout the Gospels when he sets aside the rules and expectations of the day and focuses on the people he encounters. Relationships were at the heart of his ministry and witness. We have trouble following that model when we're rushing to meet deadlines or racing to win a competition. The result can be that we ignore and even run over people as we check off our "to-do" list or jump on the podium to claim our prize.

It can even be a struggle to keep relationships front and center when we're trying to get church just right. But throughout the Gospels, Jesus seems to be saying, don't just *do* church; *be* church instead. Or as that dancer on television might say, "Don't try to be the best dancer; be a great partner."

Lost and Found

A post on Facebook of a neon motel sign in Tucumcari, New Mexico, brought a wave of memories of the summer of 1979 when I worked on the fifty-thousand-acre Chappell-Spade Ranch about fifteen miles north of that desert town. My older brother was working there full-time, and on a whim, I wrote a letter to his boss and asked for a short-term job before going back to college. "Come on out," he wrote back, and the result was a month of hard work and adventures, including the day I got lost.

It was round-up time, and a dozen men and boys spread out on horseback over the tops of some rugged mesas to find stray cattle and lead them down to a pasture for branding and doctoring. I was riding with my brother and another kid when we saw a steer move in the brush and I was sent after it. The steer got away from me, and in my pursuit of it, I got separated from the other riders. Turning back, it was as if everyone had just vanished. I was lost—as in all by myself on top of an unknown, heavily wooded mesa with no idea of how to get down or where to find the others.

After a harrowing time of looking for a way off the sheer cliffs—or even just a mesa-top view of where the other riders had gathered the herd—I leaned on my training from Scouts and decided to find a clearing and wait for help to find me. And it did. Some hours later, a four-wheel-drive truck came groaning up an eroded wash. It was the ranch cook and another woman who had brought lunch to the cowboys and had done the same for me. I was embarrassed but I was hungry, too, so I ate what they graciously provided and then followed them back down the wash and off the mesa to where the others were working.

As I trotted up, I pulled my hat down so as not to make eye contact with anyone. I rode up to my brother, leaned across his saddle, and whispered: "I'm so embarrassed; I better go home." He responded: "Don't be stupid; it's happened to all of us."

Then I was given a job to do. The rest of the day went on as if nothing had happened. I got lost, I got found, and I got back to work. That was it.

I've been lost many times since then: physically, emotionally, intellectually, spiritually. As happened on that mesa, I've felt panic, embarrassment, fear, and shame. I've tried to find my own way and just gotten more lost or gotten dangerously close to the cliffs. In most cases, the best outcomes happened when I stopped running, was still, and let myself be found.

I believe God works with us in that way, either directly or through those who God sends our way. Often, the ones who point us in the right direction have been lost themselves and have found their way back through God's directing. And now they come to us with nourishment, compassion, and directions back to where we belong. Best of all, they don't make fun or pass judgment but offer a smile that says, "good to have you back."

Dirty Feet and All

"A new command I give you: Love one another" (John 13:34a). That is the maundy—the commandment—that Jesus gave his disciples in the upper room on that last night together. It seems so simple, so logical, so natural, and yet it is perhaps the hardest commandment to keep—for me, anyway.

It's easy to like someone, to put up with, to endure, to tolerate, to accept even if just grudgingly. But to love unconditionally, unwaveringly, unhindered, unbridled? Without qualifiers, without conditions, without "yes, but . . ."? That is truly difficult, perhaps even impossible.

My thought process often goes like this: "Yes, I love that person, but I do expect him to shape up and be who I think he should be. I will put up with him until then. My love can carry me through this uncomfortable, difficult transition period until he becomes the person I find more acceptable."

But Jesus had no such qualifiers or stipulations. In fact, he gave the commandment and added, "As I have loved you, so you must love one another" (v. 34b), and he said all of that right after washing his disciples' feet. This is usually explained as an act of generosity and hospitality, but what I see and hear Jesus saying is, "Love one another—dirty feet and all." Replace "dirty feet" with whatever it is about someone that keeps you from loving them unconditionally and you get the idea.

For me, the darkness of Maundy Thursday is not the fading of the light in the church, the snuffing of the candles, the exit into the symbolic silence before Easter. Rather, it is the hardness in my heart that keeps me from loving people with dirty feet.

Widows and Orphans

My work often has me concerned about widows and orphans. No, not women and children, but that does come to mind. Let me explain.

Every year or so I find myself working on the final details of a new book, and in the jargon of book design and layout, a "widow" is the last line of a paragraph that sits at the top of a page, while an "orphan" is the first line of a paragraph at the bottom of a page. Visually, orphans are not so noticeable unless they are very short. But widows can look like a mistake.

There are typesetting techniques for resolving widows and orphans, most having to do with imperceptible adjustments to spacing between letters to pull words and sentences together into the same paragraph block. Major publishers put great care into this, especially for best-selling authors. For hands-on, self-publishing authors such as myself who don't have the software and the technical expertise, there's another method: editing. Widows and orphans can be eliminated by adding or subtracting words to make sentences longer or shorter.

It's tedious work, but it can be a good exercise for a writer because it prompts you to ask: Can I take out superfluous words and say the same thing in a more readable way? Or, can I add some words that enrich the narrative? The answer to those questions requires judgment about content and context. While the goal is a better-looking book, doing the work can result in a better written book.

So, what in the Charles Dickens does that have to do with real widows and orphans and others in need? The answer is in another book—the New Testament book of James—where we read these words: "Religion that is pure and undefiled before God, the Father, is this: to care for orphans and widows in their distress, and to keep oneself unstained by the world" (1:27).

Most of us—okay, many of us—have a surplus of wealth to share with those who have little. But we like our stuff. We work hard for our stuff. We like what our stuff says about us: it creates a narrative of who we are and what we have accomplished. We like it when our life reads like a good book.

But if we're reading that other book—and comprehending the subplot that is not so hidden between the lines—we know we are called to help those in need. That requires some editing of our lives: cutting out what is not truly needed so we can give from our abundance to those with little, or expanding our lives to give our time and energy to causes that bring relief. In doing so, we help write the story of the kingdom of God on earth as it is in heaven; we add chapters of a more abundant life to people whose stories are headed toward an ending that we wouldn't want for ourselves.

In editing our lives for the good of others, we end up with a better narrative of who we are; more healthy and holy. A lot of that stuff we want—and the pursuit of it—can have a way of staining us, as James suggests. And who really wants that when the last chapter of their life is read?

Freewheeling Love

The card inside the box of flowers read: "From your loving husband. I will keep you forever. You make my whole self smile. I couldn't trade you for anything in the world."

The flowers were delivered to our front porch by mistake, but at first we opened them thinking they were sent to LeAnn as a "get well soon" gift following her eye surgery. But then we read the card and checked the address on the box. The number was right, but the street name was wrong; the correct destination was a boutique hotel near downtown Dallas. I called the flower company and talked through the mistake and learned that the flowers were ordered by a man who was celebrating his anniversary with his wife. We were told, "Keep the flowers and we'll send them a new box."

With that settled, we enjoyed the flowers—red roses mixed with white calla lilies—for a full week. But, something about the card still bothered me. It was that word "couldn't." Maybe I'm being too picky, but "couldn't trade you for anything in the world" is not the same thing as "wouldn't trade you for anything in the world." "Couldn't" sounds like one might trade if there was not an impediment or deterrence of some sort. "Wouldn't" sounds like the world is open to any kind of wheeling and dealing, and yet you wouldn't trade. One sounds like captured love; the other sounds like unleashed love—freewheeling love.

Freewheeling love sounds like the relationship that God wants with us—one that is freewheeling because it's based on free will. We're not tied down where we can't stray; we're free to come and go, but we don't want to go because the love is so strong and real. And if we do stray, we're free to come back into God's loving arms where we're told, "I will keep you forever. You make my whole self smile. I wouldn't trade you for anything."

I hope the anniversary couple got their flowers. I say that because we got a second delivery. This time the driver sensed an error and rang our doorbell instead of just leaving the flowers on the porch. When I told him it was a mistake, again, and explained the correct address, I added, "I know that couple will appreciate getting their flowers." The driver looked at his watch and said, "Not from me, not tonight." I don't know if he couldn't deliver the flowers, or if he just wouldn't.

Flowers or no flowers, I hope the anniversary couple had a great celebration. More than that, I pray they have a wonderful life together. I wish them a life of freewheeling love.

Christmas Reunion

At the Christmas Eve worship service, the student choir sang "A Star," a beautiful piece with these words: "A star of heavenly design, revealing hope to mankind."[4] Afterward, the students came down out of the choir loft and dispersed into the pews. Later, when it was time to walk down to the front of the church for Communion, I noticed that the students weren't clumped together as they usually are. On this night, they walked down the aisles with their families—sons and daughters united with mothers and fathers.

I saw in that moment a vision of heaven, where loved ones are reunited at the table of the Lord. That, my friends, is the hope of Christmas, the reason for the season.

REFERENCES

Family and Friends: Flesh and Blood

[1]"And I Love You So." Words and Music by Don McLean. Copyright (c) 1970, 1972 BENNY BIRD CO., INC. Copyright Renewed. All Rights Controlled and Administered by SONGS OF UNIVERSAL, INC. All Rights Reserved Used by Permission. *Reprinted by Permission of Hal Leonard LLC.*

[2]"Feels Like Home." Words and Music by RANDY NEWMAN. Copyright © 1996 RANDY NEWMAN MUSIC (ASCAP). All Rights Reserved. Used By Permission of ALFRED MUSIC.

Neighbors: Next Door and Down the Street

[1]Fred Rogers, *The World According to Mr. Rogers* (Hyperion Books, 2003), 167.

[2]"Blessing of the Fleet" is a long-used prayer with many variations and no definitive origin.

[3]Prayer by Diann Neu, D. Min, Co-director of The Women's Alliance for Theology, Ethics, and Ritual (WATER), from *Imaging the Word: An Arts and Lectionary Resource*, vol. 1 (United Church Press, 1994), 37.

The Human Family: Across Town and Around the Globe

[1]Kathleen Thomerson, "I Want to Walk as a Child of the Light, © 1970, 1975 Celebration. Used by permission of the Community of Celebration. All rights reserved.

[2]Thomas A. Dorsey, "Precious Lord, Take My Hand," 1932.

[3]William Whiting, "Eternal Father, Strong to Save," 1860.

[4]Bob Thiele (as George Douglas) and George David Weiss, "What a Wonderful World."

[5]"Hello in There." Words and Music by JOHN PRINE. Copyright © 1970 (Renewed) WALDEN MUSIC, INC. and SOUR GRAPES MUSIC, INC. All Rights Administered by WALDEN MUSIC, INC. All Rights Reserved. Used By Permission of ALFRED MUSIC.

Church and the Kingdom: Kindred Spirits

[1]"Brown Eyed Girl." Words and Music by Van Morrison. Copyright (c) 1967 UNIVERSAL MUSIC PUBLISHING INTERNATIONAL LTD. Copyright Renewed. All Rights for the U.S. and Canada Controlled and Administered by UNIVERSAL—SONGS OF POLYGRAM INTERNATIONAL, INC. All Rights Reserved. Used by Permission. *Reprinted by Permission of Hal Leonard LLC.*

[2]*The Dallas Morning News* (Sept. 7, 2013).

[3]Howard Thurman, "The Work of Christmas" from *The Mood of Christmas and Other Celebrations* (Friends United Press, 1985).

[4]Pepper Choplin, "A Star." Composed by Pepper Choplin. 12 pages. Purifoy Publishing Company #10/1048 (Jan. 1, 1971).

ABOUT THE AUTHOR

Published Contributions

American Builders Quarterly
American Cranes & Transport
Austin Magazine
Baptist News Global
Baylor Arts & Sciences Magazine
Branson: On-Stage in the Ozarks
Canadian Builders Quarterly
Commercial Aviation Report
Convenience Store News
Cowboys & Indians
Dallas Business Journal
Dallas Magazine
Dallas Style & Design
Dallas/Fort Worth Then and Now
Dallas: Proud Heritage, Shining Future
Green Building & Design
Hispanic Business Magazine

Inmotion
Lifting & Moving the World
McLane Company: The First One Hundred Years,
    1894–1994
Nation's Building News
New American Luxury
Texas Business
Texas Construction Magazine
Texas Sports
Texas: A State for All
The Baylor Lariat
The Baylor Line
The Creatives Magazine
The Dallas Morning News
The New York Times
Vitality
Waco Tribune-Herald

Books by Jeff Hampton

Grandpa Jack
Jonah Prophet: An Allegory on the Old Testament Tale
The Snowman Uprising on Hickory Lane
When the Light Returned to Main Street
Aransas Morning
Aransas Evening
When the Light Returned to Main Street (2nd ed.)

Awards and Honors

Katie Award – Press Club of Dallas
Silver Quill – International Association of Business Communicators
Bronze Anvil – Public Relations Society of America
Best of Texas – Texas Public Relations Association
Blue Pencil Award – National Association of Government Communicators
AdWheel – American Public Transportation Association
Compass Award – Transportation Marketing and Communications Association

Contact

Jeff Hampton | Jefton@aol.com | 214-578-4611
901 W. Avenue E, Garland, TX 75040
www.jeffhamptonwriter.com

CPSIA information can be obtained
at www.ICGtesting.com
Printed in the USA
BVHW041537250321
603416BV00007B/844

9 781635 281323